MW01005230

COCKTAIL BOOTHBY'S

AMERICAN BARTENDER

STANDARD | AUTHORITY.

THE ONLY PRACTICAL TREATISE ON THE
ART OF MIXOLOGY PUBLISHED.

CONTAINING

Nearly Four Hundred Standard Recipes for the Mixing
of Absinthes, Cocktails, Coolers, Cobblers, Crustas,
Fixes, Flips, Fizzes, Hot Drinks, Lemonades,
Punches, Sangarees, Shakes, Toddies, etc.;

ALSO

MUCH VALUABLE INFORMATION RELATING TO THE RETAIL LIQUOR
BUSINESS.

1891.

BY WILLIAM T. BOOTHBY

THE NEW ANCHOR DISTILLING EDITION
EDITED BY DAVID BURKHART
2009

FOREWORD BY FRITZ MAYTAG
AND DAVID BURKHART

ANCHOR DISTILLING ~ SAN FRANCISCO

Published by Anchor Distilling
1705 Mariposa Street
San Francisco, California 94107 USA
Tel 415.863.8350, Fax 415.552.7094
www.anchordistilling.com

ISBN-13: 978-0-9822473-3-4
Library of Congress Control Number: 2009903446

Originally printed in San Francisco in 1891 by
H. S. Crocker Company

The New Anchor Distilling Edition
Copyright © 2009
All rights reserved. Published 2009

Printed in Canada by Hemlock Printers on acid-free archival paper.

Anchor Distilling gratefully acknowledges the California Historical Society,
San Francisco, for permission to reproduce the original cover and contents
of the first edition of *Cocktail Boothby's American Bartender*.

N.B.: Anchor Distilling is not responsible for the recipes, ingredients, secrets revealed,
suggestions, commandments, or advice in *Cocktail Boothby's American Bartender*, or for
any adverse reactions that may result from their use. If you have food allergies or other
health concerns, consult your physician.

HON. WILLIAM THOMAS BOOTHBY
NOVEMBER 10, 1862 – AUGUST 4, 1930

Photograph (after 1907) courtesy of the California Historical Society, San Francisco.
Autographed on June 17, 1920, the day of his beloved mother's funeral.

"I have seen purer liquors, better segars, finer tobacco, truer guns
and pistols, larger dirks and bowie knives, and prettier courtezans here, than
in any other place I have ever visited; and it is my unbiased opinion that
California can and does furnish the best bad things that are obtainable in America."

–HINTON R. HELPER, *The Land of Gold: Reality Versus Fiction* (1855)

BAR-ROOM IN CALIFORNIA.

ILLUSTRATION (c. 1854) BY FRANK MARRYAT,
as engraved in his Mountains and Molehills or Recollections of a Burnt Journal *(1855)*.
Courtesy of David Burkhart.

FOREWORD

"THERE IS NO ONE IN SUCH A HURRY AS A CALIFORNIAN, but he has always time to take a drink." So wrote gold rush journalist Frank Marryat, who arrived at the mouth of the bay of San Francisco on June 14, 1850. In those days, thirsty miners beelined from the assayer's office to their favorite saloon. They had many choices. In 1853, according to historian Hubert Howe Bancroft, "there were in San Francisco 537 places where liquor was sold, 46 of which were public gambling houses, 743 bartenders officiating. No wonder that hard times set in."

The lavish decor of these barrooms often belied the dangers within, from low-caliber spirits to high-caliber pistols. Savvy bartenders had an easy solution for the latter. Strategically positioned beneath the mahogany were sandbags, behind which they could take cover whenever *shots poured* escalated to *shots fired*.

Gold rush San Francisco was a wellspring of libationary delights. According to Marryat, its bartenders were artists in their profession, mixing everything from Queen Charlottes to Stone Fences. The creativity, skill, and showmanship of these pioneer mixologists were not lost even on Bancroft, the relatively sober chronicler of all things Californian:

> "The apt and chameleon-like bar-keeper, who could adapt himself to the color and moods of every customer, though not a proprietor, was a person of no mean consequence. Studying his business as a profession he rose in it, ennobling himself while he ennobled his occupation, as he acquired skill. With practice his clumsy fingers became pliable, and bottles and glasses flew from shelf, hand, and counter in orderly confusion.
>
> "Decanters tipped their several ingredients into the forming compound with magic nicety, and cascades of brilliant liquids poured from glass to glass held at arm's length with the precision of a rock-bound cataract [waterfall]. Nor was the profession restricted in its advancement to mere mechanical skill. Ingenuity was displayed in concocting new nectar, and soon a long list of delicious beverages became as household words."

Sportsman/travel writer Francis Francis penned a wry paean to the nobility of these beverages for the *Nineteenth Century*. To Francis, the cocktail was "drinking etherealised" and its *imbiber* the "true artist":

> "The analytic skill of a chemist marks his swift and unerring detection of the very faintest dissonance in the harmony of the ingredients that compose his beverage. He has an antidote to dispel, a tonic to induce every mood and humour that man knows. Endless variety rewards a single-hearted devotion to cocktails; whilst the refinement and artistic spirit that may be displayed in such an attachment, redeem it from intemperance.... A cocktail hath the soul of wit, it is brief. It is a jest, a bon-mot, happy thought, a gibe, a word of sympathy, a tear, an inspiration, a short prayer."

In 1849, New Haven–born bartender Jerry Thomas made the first of several trips to California. By 1862, the peripatetic mixologist had already served as the "Jupiter Olympus of the bar" at the Metropolitan Hotel, New York, and the "presiding deity" at the Planter's House, St. Louis. The fanciful titles appear in the preface to his *How to Mix Drinks, or the Bon-Vivant's Companion*, published that year. It is a compilation of recipes—some of dubious provenance—from the Blue Blazer to the Tom and Jerry. The year 1862 was also when Sarah Elenor Boothby gave birth in San Francisco to a native son that would become known as Cocktail Bill.

Sarah (née Morse, 1834–1920) hailed from Rochester, New York. Her Maine-born husband was William Lord Boothby (1832–1885). A teamster for most of his working life, he was also a San Francisco firefighter in the mid-1850s, a baker, and a restaurateur. Their first son, David, was born in 1856. William Thomas Boothby was born in San Francisco on November 10, 1862.

WILLIAM L. BOOTHBY BUSINESS CARD, c. 1873.
From the Boothby scrapbook, courtesy of the California Historical Society.
WILLIAM T. BOOTHBY BUSINESS CARD, c. 1882.

Young Bill worked as a tailor, as a clerk, and as a conductor for the Central Railroad (a local street railway). William L. died on February 16, 1885. By then, William T. had already opened "Boothby's Agency," in the Elite Building (838 Market). It was undoubtedly the only place in town where one could rent a flat—from William—and, for five dollars, purchase Dr. Gray's Electric Belt ("Instantly relieve and speedily cure ACHES, PAINS, NERVOUSNESS and WEAKNESS of both sexes")—from his mother. By early 1887, the entreprenurial Sarah Boothby had her own coffee saloon on Market Street. Over the years, she collaborated with her son William in several bakery and restaurant ventures. Sarah also owned a prune orchard near Mountain View. After the 1906 San Francisco earthquake, she moved to Berkeley. In 1915, the "hale and hearty" eighty-one-year-old endorsed a rheumatism cure called Akoz. It must have worked. The still-venturesome forty-niner celebrated five more birthdays.

Critical to the development of the showmanship that W. T. Boothby exhibited behind the bar later in life was his early experience onstage as a vaudevillian. A rare scrapbook at the California Historical Society sheds light on William and his brother, David's, days as itinerant performers. David, a talented actor and impressionist, was also a "strict prohibitionist," according to one newspaper clipping. He died at age twenty-seven, while touring in Montana with singer/danceuse Katie Putnam's troupe. Most of William's theatrical work was on the road with the Vigor of Life Minstrel Co. in 1886 and 1887.

The Vigor of Life was a medicinal remedy created in 1871 by a Chicagoan, Dr. William A. Johnson. New York–born Palmer Clark, who first arrived in California in 1852, came into possession of the copyright and began using minstrel shows to promote his product: "A purely 'vegetable' compound capable of getting the drop on all diseases except consumption and hydrophobia," wrote one enthusiastic journalist. "The Great Boothby" ("King of Terpsichore") was a featured writer and performer with the Vigor of Life troupe, based in Sacramento. "The

"AND ALL IT COSTS IS
A DOLLAR A BOTTLE."
From the Boothby scrapbook, courtesy
of the California Historical Society.

Inimitable" W. T. Boothby's "artistic pedal manipulations" and "poetry of motion personified" were legendary, or at least billed as such. His "great specialty" was dancing a jig while balancing a tumbler of water on his head. The Boothby scrapbook's clippings and handbills indicate that young William traveled throughout California and as far east as Montana and Wyoming with this merry minstrel band.

According to William, he traveled extensively—tending bar in New York, Chicago, Philadelphia, New Orleans, and Kansas City. All that is known with any degree of certainty is that his earliest bartending experience in California came in the late 1880s, at Byron Hot Springs (the "Carlsbad of the West," about seventy miles east of San Francisco) and at a San Francisco saloon on Geary Street called the Silver Palace. Letters of recommendation in the Boothby scrapbook attest to his skill, integrity, diligence, and sobriety.

HOTEL RAFAEL: CLUB HOUSE (Artotype, Britton & Rey, lithographers, published July 4, 1890). Courtesy of Department of Special Collections and University Archives, Stanford University Libraries. *The Club House had its own billiard room, wine cellar, barroom, and presiding deity: Cocktail Boothby.*

HOTEL RAFAEL: THE HOTEL (Artotype, Britton & Rey, lithographers, published July 4, 1890). Courtesy of Department of Special Collections and University Archives, Stanford University Libraries. *Built in 1888 near the intersection of Belle and Grand avenues, San Rafael's fashionable resort hotel burned in 1928. Its architect was Thomas J. Welsh (1845–1918), who also designed San Francisco's Sacred Heart Church and Santa Cruz's Golden Gate Villa.*

In 1891, the *San Francisco Chronicle* serialized Bret Harte's *A "First Family" of Tasajara*. The quintessentially Californian novel offered the definition of a San Francisco excursion: "A dusty drive with a cocktail at the end of it." By that time, Boothby was mixing cocktails at the Hotel Rafael Club House, where the proud young author of *Cocktail Boothby's American Bartender* served as the self-proclaimed "presiding deity" (see Jerry Thomas, above). The San Rafael hotel, which opened in the summer of 1888, was the epitome of Victorian opulence. In 1896, Baron and Baroness von Schroeder turned down an offer of $150,000 for it from San Francisco millionaire Walter Hobart.

In an 1882 article on the "art of intellectual tippling," the *San Francisco Chronicle* posited that "of the thousand and one vocations by which men earn an honest crust and keep themselves out of San Quentin, the lot of the modest 'barkeep' is not the most inglorious." With a nod to David Broderick's and James C. Flood's mixological beginnings, the *Chronicle* noted that the noble bartender "has been the pioneer in every settlement since the days of gold, and has dispensed, along with much indifferent refreshment, every official emolument from a fireman's badge to the Senatorial togs." By 1894, Cocktail Bill had become a well-known author and mixologist, familiar to patrons of the Parker House, at Geary and Stockton. It was time for a new venture: politics.

On November 6, 1894, Adolph Sutro was elected mayor of San Francisco and William T. Boothby was elected to the California State Assembly. He credited the unanimous support of San Francisco's liquor dealers for this, his first—and only—political triumph (although, in 1904, he was elected president of the Unity Club,

CANDIDATE BOOTHBY *in 1894, as depicted in the* San Francisco Chronicle.

Cor. Stockton

WM. T. BOOTHBY. Cocktail Boothby
Expert Mixologist

GEARY ST.—NORTH SIDE

WM. T. BOOTHBY   TELEPHONE, BLACK 1403   SMILEY GARVIN

STRAIGHT GOODS

COCKTAILS
OUR
SPECIALTY

The Parker House
Cafe and Bar

200 STOCKTON STREET
CORNER GEARY

San Francisco, Cal.

PRIVATE ENTRANCE, GEARY ST.

▲ FROM *THE ILLUSTRATED DIRECTORY: A MONTHLY MAGAZINE OF AMERICAN CITIES* (Vol. I, No. 9, October 1895). Courtesy of the California History Room, California State Library, Sacramento, California. *Note the Cocktail Boothby imagery.*

◀ BUSINESS CARD, c. 1894. From the Boothby scrapbook, courtesy of the California Historical Society.

a protective association for members of the "white apron fraternity"). Boothby represented the 43rd District for one term—from January 7 to March 16, 1895—authored several bills, and was known forever after as the *Honorable* Wm. T. (Cocktail) Boothby. "The wise man is he," opined Rudyard Kipling in 1889, "who, keeping a liquor-saloon and judiciously dispensing drinks, knows how to retain within arm's reach a block of men who will vote for or against anything under the canopy of Heaven."

After his election, Boothby was approached by an anti-suffragist, who asked him to take a stand against a woman's right to vote. "Madam," replied the newly elected representative of San Francisco's seedy "Tenderloin," "it is impossible for me to do so. The district I represent in San Francisco is so thickly populated by women that if I can only secure suffrage for them I will be all right politically the rest of my days."

After the 1906 earthquake and fire, Boothby presided—with the less Olympian title of "premier mixologist"—at the Pacific Buffet, situated in the Pacific Building, at 4th and Market. The Louis Sullivan–esque edifice still stands today. He also bartended at the Fairmont Hotel. But his artistry particularly delighted guests of the new Palace Hotel, which opened in 1909. "They were all aces at that mahogany, and Bill was the ace of aces," wrote a nostalgic editor for the *San Francisco Recorder* in 1934. "To see him rotating three cocktail glasses between the fingers of his left hand while measuring a jigger of gin or vermouth [we prefer the former] with the right was to witness a masterpiece of art in the making."

In 1911, Waldemar Young—the Herb Caen of his day—recounted an amusing story about a busy bartender and a bibulous barfly.

"'Cocktail Billy' Boothby is a familiar figure behind the bars of the big San Francisco hotels and has been for a time long in the memory of man. They know him at the Fairmont and at the Palace—those men, at least, who go to the bar during the witching hour that precedes dinner, when 'Cocktail Billy' is in his element, dealing out over the polished mahogany his spurs to jaded appetites.

"Just at present 'Cocktail Billy' divides his working hours among the Fairmont, the Palace and a downtown bar which is situate midway between these associated hostelries. He is 'extra man' at each place, filling out his eight-hour shift in installments at each oasis.

"It so happened recently that a visitor to this fair city ('fair' city isn't bad at all, eh?) dropped into the Fairmont bar early in the afternoon to pour something cool and tasty on the heated coppers. 'Cocktail Billy' it was who served him, and the man liked so well what he received that he called for another. Then he went on about his business rejoicing.

"Down the Powell-street hill came the visitor. Certain business had to be transacted in the Flood building, and this required an hour or more. When he emerged 'Cocktail Billy' had changed his base of operations and was at work in the downtown bar. The visitor dropped in for a drink. 'Cocktail Billy' greeted him smilingly. The man staggered back.

"'I've seen you somewhere before,' he said.

"'I don't think so, sir,' said Billy.

"'Have you got a brother working at the Fairmont?'

"'No, sir.'

"'Most curious, most curious,' muttered the visitor, taking his drink.

"Other business detained the visitor around town for another hour, when he wound up at the Crocker building, opposite the Palace. Dropping over to the Palace, it was, of course, 'Cocktail Billy' who leaned with a smile over the bar to take his order.

"The man stared aghast. 'Have YOU got a brother working at the Fairmont?' he demanded.

"'No, sir, not I,' answered Billy. 'What will you have?'

"'Not a thing!' moaned the visitor, pale to the lips. 'When I get as bad as this it's time to quit. I'm through forever!'"

The Boothby Cocktail—also known as the Boothby Manhattan—was invented by Bill when he was head bartender at the Palace Hotel. According to a 1930 article in the *San Francisco Chronicle*, "it consisted of a delectable Manhattan, with a champagne float—a drink that never the gods of high Olympus quaffed." The recipe appears under "MANHATTAN, BOOTHBY" in a posthumous edition of Boothby's book, which was published in November 1930. We recommend our single-malt rye for this San Francisco classic.

THE BOOTHBY COCKTAIL

Whisky ....²⁄₃ jigger	Orange Bitters ....2 dashes
Italian Vermouth ..... ¹⁄₃ jigger	Angostura Bitters ..... 2 drops

Stir well with ice, strain into chilled cocktail glass, add Maraschino cherry, float on 1 spoon of champagne and serve.

With the outbreak of World War I came a new Boothby creation. In November 1914, the *Oakland Tribune* described William's attempt at mixological détente:

"'Cocktail Bill' Boothby, the literary mixologist of the Palace, was listening to a heated argument between a German and a Frenchman in the wineroom the other afternoon. In the interests of neutrality he asked the debaters to try the latest cocktail of the hotel. They were willing. While they were exchanging angry words and threats Boothby mixed a cocktail with the following ingredients: English gin, Russian vodka, German kummel, Hungarian apricot brandy, Italian Vermouth brandy, manufactured in Ghent, Belgium, and a dash of French Amer Picon. The German and the Frenchman stopped their argument long enough to try the cocktail. They liked it and ordered another, and then a third, and then a fourth. Their argument became less and less heated.

"'What do you call that new drink?' asked the German.

"'Peace cocktail,' replied Boothby.

"The German and the Frenchman departed arm in arm."

Rather than taking sides, Boothby had creatively applied the wise advice of Victor Reiter, the Palace's longtime maître d'hôtel: "The man who keeps his mouth shut has the rest of us guessing." And he may have created the first vodka cocktail.

Everything changed on January 16, 1920, although—according to Will Rogers— "Prohibition is better than no liquor at all." Boothby made the best of it. On St. Valentine's Day, 1921, he was arrested during a raid of the Orpheum Annex on O'Farrell. He pled guilty in federal court to violation of the Volstead Act and was fined $250. It was not his first run-in with the law. In 1894, Boothby had been arrested for scalping tickets to the Midwinter Fair in Golden Gate Park. All in all, "Prohibition hit Bill rather badly," eulogized the *San Francisco News*. The aging bartender "continued his mixing activities by dispensing

"Bar Room–Palace Hotel. The best people from
all over the world have at one time or another rested their tired feet
on the highly polished brass rail of this bar counter.
I've been there myself."

Above the back bar is Maxfield Parrish's 7 x 16–foot
mural, *The Pied Piper*, commissioned for San Francisco's
new Palace Hotel in 1909. Parrish used himself as the
model for Hamelin's most famous musician. Among the
twenty-seven children depicted are two of Parrish's own:
Dillwyn and Maxfield Jr. The artist offered sage advice to
those tending bar beneath his masterpiece: "When customers
can no longer tell how many children they can count on
the mural, send them home to their families."

In 1913, Boothby was credited with saving *The Pied Piper*
from an untimely demise. An overzealous janitor, after
thoroughly cleaning the Palace Buffet's woodwork, trained
his vacuum cleaner on Parrish's priceless canvas. Boothby
walked in just in time. Instead of confronting the culprit
directly, the quick-thinking bartender simply turned off
the electricity. No damage was done, and the colorful mural
still hangs at the Palace Hotel today.

HON. WM. T. (COCKTAIL) BOOTHBY POSTCARD, c. 1929.
Courtesy of the California Historical Society.

soft drinks at the Olympic Club." He also served as steward at the Hotel St. Francis for the Far Western Travelers Club. On August 4, 1930, after a yearlong battle with cancer, William T. Boothby died at his San Francisco home. The city's bons vivants grieved, although legally forbidden to drink to his memory.

Cocktail Boothby's American Bartender was, by his own account, first compiled and published in 1890. Although Boothby copyrighted his book on October 14 of that year, the US Copyright Office did not receive its copies of the charming and informative guide (printed in 1891) until April 23, 1891. In his 1908 edition, Boothby writes that a total of "three editions, numbering over 50,000 copies were sold previous to the San Francisco fire, which destroyed the plates and lithographs, together with the stock on hand." Today, only two known copies of Boothby's first edition remain.

This new Anchor Distilling edition is a complete and meticulous reproduction of the first edition of *Cocktail Boothby's American Bartender*. The handsome copy we used, printed in 1891, is at the California Historical Society, San Francisco. Pasted into the back of the book are carbon copies of four typewritten pages of recipes (see "ADENDA" [*sic*]), which we have included in this new edition. Seventeen of these drinks made the cut for Boothby's 1908 edition, which begs the obvious but unanswered question: Could this have been his own copy? For comparison, we have also included a handwritten version of the addenda, found tucked into a copy of Boothby's 1900 edition.

Boothby's introduction is refreshingly iconoclastic, with a dash of California bravado. His Ten Commandments are as relevant today as they are quaint. Although he eschewed brand names in these early recipes, Boothby happily accepted advertising, including eight ads for champagne. Ironically, Cocktail Bill was fond of this sparkling doggerel:

> "Here's to Champagne, the drink divine
> That makes us forget our troubles,
> It's made of a dollar's worth of wine
> And four dollars' worth of bubbles."

Boothby's book is as promised: a practical guidebook that, even today, merits a spot on both back bar and bookshelf. However, we cannot in this century endorse his "valuable secrets for liquor dealers," nor accept credit or blame for the restorative or deleterious effects of his alchemic potions!

Salient for distillers and mixologists alike is the distinction that Boothby makes between "Holland" gin—also known as genever, it was used in the earliest mixed drinks that called for gin—and "Old Tom." Interestingly, his martini recipe predates the ascendancy of modern distilled dry gin. Not until the addenda do we see recipes that make use of this so-called "English" gin. In addition to the many genever recipes in this book (e.g., #23), we offer one here from his 1908 edition. We recommend our Genevieve® Genever-Style Gin for this old-fashioned San Francisco cocktail—and any new genever recipes that it might inspire.

BOOTHBY'S HOLLAND GIN COCKTAIL

Into a mixing glass place some cracked ice, a teaspoonful of gum syrup*,
a dash of Boonekamp bitters, a dash of Orange bitters,
three drops of Absinthe, and a jigger of good Holland gin.
Agitate briskly, strain, squeeze a piece of lemon rind over the top, and serve.
N.B.—Peychaud's Aromatic Bitter Cordial, a New Orleans product,
is highly recommended as a substitute for Boonekamp bitters,
and is universally used with Holland gin in the Southern States.

*See recipe #361. David Wondrich offers a simple modern recipe for gum syrup in *Imbibe!*,
his wonderful book about Jerry Thomas. Wondrich suggests dissolving two pounds
of white sugar or demerara sugar in one pint of water over low heat. Allow it to cool, adding
½ ounce grain alcohol or 1 ounce vodka as a preservative. Use immediately or refrigerate.

Of course, with all of Cocktail Bill's recipes—from the Breck and Brace to Pacific-Union Club Punch—the proof of the pudding is in the imbibing.

What was San Francisco like in Boothby's day? Bombay-born Rudyard Kipling took the pulse of Cocktail Bill's San Francisco in 1889. That year, the twenty-three-year-old Kipling came to California to *see the elephant*. This special phrase, according to historian J. S. "Jim" Holliday, was "used by almost every gold rush diarist." Although it "had been a part of the American language before 1849, it took on a poignant meaning for the tens of thousands who experienced getting to California and then life in the mining camps." Perhaps the best description of its origin may be found in *A Dictionary of Slang, Jargon & Cant*, published the same year as Kipling's California sojourn: "The phrase seems to have originated in an old ballad of a farmer who, while driving his mare along the highway, met with a showman's elephant, which knocked him over, and spilt his milk and destroyed his eggs. The farmer consoled himself for his loss by reflecting that he had at least 'seen the elephant.'"

For Kipling, the elephant was the California he had read about in the prose and poetry of Bret Harte. But during Kipling's eighteen short days in San Francisco, he saw neither the serenity nor the indifference that Harte ascribed so poetically to the city "at the Western Gate." Instead, Kipling found "rare and curious drinks at more than one bar," beautiful women, bad accents, free lunches, bunco-steerers, Button Punch ("compounded of the shavings of cherubs' wings, the glory of a tropical dawn, the red clouds of sunset, and fragments of lost epics by dead masters"), the Palace Hotel, hills, cable cars, and the Cliff House. He distilled the essence of the "rush and whirl" of San Francisco in a letter to a dear friend: "There is no other place like it. Reckless and roaring like nothing you ever saw. The men make money and 'break up' with a rush that goes to your head. Everything is done on a large scale, even the coins are not small."

This gold rush recklessness, anything-is-possible risk taking, unbridled confidence, and robust optimism are fundamental to what historian Kevin Starr cogently calls California's DNA code. Jim Holliday saw its manifestation in Kipling's vivid descriptions of San Francisco. Gold was the catalyst, Holliday tells us: "No other state, no nation, has had such a beginning, such a period of adolescent success and freedom. Think what it has meant to California's image, its spirit, its psyche to have the Forty-niners as heroes, as Founding Fathers—compared to the Pilgrims. To have wild, rambunctious, better yet, sinful San Francisco as the Mother City."

We call our "sinful" experiments at Anchor Distilling essays, from the French word meaning "to try." (Both "essay" and "assay"—as in the assaying of gold—are derived from the Latin verb meaning "to weigh.") In Jack London's *Sea Wolf*, for example, the fiendish Captain Wolf Larsen "essays to" write his dying words. Long ago, essays were written *at* subjects, rather than *on* them. In his *Two Years Before the Mast*, Richard Henry Dana Jr. "essays at" the work of a sailor. Essays in this sense of the word involve newness, creativity, and risk. Today, our California DNA compels the pioneer in us to seek the new, to create, to risk, to try.

Cocktail Boothby's American Bartender is more than a charming little collection of recipes by a beloved fin de siècle mixologist. Boothby's guide is a venture taken, an opportunity seized, a successful essay. Though only a small piece of San Francisco's richly storied puzzle, Cocktail Bill's book is an exemplary expression of the California dream. For in creating it, this mixological prospector risked a most valuable treasure: his reputation.

Special thanks to David Crosson and the superb staff at the California Historical Society; The Bancroft Library, University of California, Berkeley; the California State Archives; the California State Library; the Hastings Law Library; the Marin History Museum; the San Francisco Public Library; the Shields Library, University of California, Davis; The Society of California Pioneers; Stanford University Libraries; David Wondrich; John C. Burton; Creative Solutions; Elaine Kwong Design; Amyx Photography; and Hemlock Printers for their help in re-creating this uniquely San Franciscan book. Dutch Cocktails (see recipe #21) all 'round!

Fritz Maytag and David Burkhart
Anchor Distilling, San Francisco
April 2009

Wm. T. Boothby

Dec. 15th 1885.

THE BOOTHBY SCRAPBOOK

*is a family album. It contains photographs, handbills, business cards, newspaper clippings,
and other ephemera from the early careers of William T. and David N. Boothby (a third child died
in infancy). It also contains letters of recommendation from some of Cocktail Bill's employers.*

Courtesy of the California Historical Society.

TRADE CARD. Courtesy of David Burkhart.

"The 'Vigor of Life Concert Troupe' has been giving open air concerts on our streets the past two nights. They travel in a four horse vehicle, with handsome bays and a fine wagon, and the company, four in number, gives a first class vocal and instrumental concert, while the proprietor sells the 'Vigor.' Most traveling medicine performances are snide, but this is very far from being so."

–From a newspaper clipping in the Boothby scrapbook.

EARLY BOTTLE.
Courtesy of David Burkhart.

Note the Boothby portrait, ►
which he later used on the title
page of his *American Bartender*.

DON'T MISS IT!

"Dip Me Again in the Golden Sea."

THURSDAY EVENING, APRIL 29, 1886.

Opera House, Napa.

THE RENOWNED
"VIGOR OF LIFE"

Concert and Minstrel Co.

Will give one of their Special Hall Shows. Two hours of solid fun,
consisting of
QUARTETTS, DUETS, TRIOS, BALLADS, COMIC SONGS, ETC.

Their Specialties Consist of

SKETCHES, FARCES, ETC.

THE INIMITABLE
W. T. BOOTHBY, Will keep the audience in a roar of laughter in his
Hebrew, Dutch and Negro Delineations; also, challenges any one in Jig Dancing

Dr. FULLER, In his Original Yankee Character Acts, is second to none.

Not least **Messrs. CODDINGTON & JOINER,**
In British eccentricities, will surely please all.

Gentlemanly ushers and strict order is our motto.

ADMISSION - - - - - - - **25 Cents.**
Children under 12 years, accompanied by parents, admitted free.
NO EXTRA CHARGE FOR RESERVED SEATS. No postponement on
account of weather. Doors open at 7 o'clock, commences at 8.

Respectfully,
Dr. PALMER CLARK,
Proprietor Vigor of Life Concert Troupe.

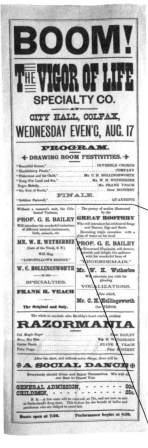

BOOM!

THE VIGOR OF LIFE
SPECIALTY CO.
—AT—
CITY HALL, COLFAX,
WEDNESDAY EVEN'G, AUG. 17

PROGRAM.
→ DRAWING ROOM FESTIVITIES. →

"Beautiful Sunset,"........................INVISIBLE CHORUS
Mons. Bal Rye,".................................COMPANY
"Fisherman and his Child,"..........Mr. C. H. HOLLINGSWORTH
"King O'er Land and Sea,".........Mr. W. H. WETHERBEE
Negro Melody,..................................Mr. FRANK VEACH
"Six Foot of Earth,"............................Prof. BOOTHBY

FINALE.

"Soldiers Farewell,"..............................QUARTETTE

Without a moment's wait, the Cele-   The poetry of motion illustrated
brated Violinist,   by the

PROF. G. E. BAILEY   **GREAT BOOTHBY**
Will introduce his wonderful imitations   Who will introduce his celebrated Songs
of different musical instruments,   and Dances, Jigs and Reels.
birds, animals, etc.   Executing triple execution · with a
                                          glass of water on his head.
MR. W. H. WETHERBEE
(Late of the Tivoli, S. F.)   **PROF. G. E. BAILEY**
Will Sing   The Renowned Illusionist, will deceive,
—"LONGFELLOW'S BRIDGE"—   astonish and delight the audience
                                   with his wonderful feats of
W. C. HOLLINGSWORTH   "LEGERDEMAIN."
—IN HIS—
SPECIALTIES.   **Mr. W. H. Wetherbee**
                                  Will entertain you with his
FRANK H. VEACH   pleasing
The Original and Only.   VOCALIZATIONS.
                                  After which,
The whole to conclude with Boothby's heart-rending   **Mr. C. H. Hollingsworth**
entitled   Our TENOR.

RAZORMANIA

Col. Maple Sugar...............................Prof. BAILEY
Mons. Bal Rye..................................Wm. H. WETHERBEE
Oyster Smith..................................FRANK H. VEACH
Peter Props..................................Prof. BOOTHBY

After the show, and without extra charge, there will be

⊕ A SOCIAL DANCE ⊕

Everybody should Come and Enjoy Themselves. We will do
our Best to Please You.

GENERAL ADMISSION, - - - - - 50c
CHILDREN, - - - - - - - 25c

N. B.—A few seats will be reserved, at 75c, and are now on sale
at Rutherford's drug store. This is done for the benefit of ladies and
gentlemen who are obliged to come late.

Doors open at 7:30.   Performance begins at 8:30.

The poetry of motion illustrated
by the

GREAT BOOTHBY

Who will introduce his celebrated Songs
and Dances, Jigs and Reels.

Executing triple execution with a
glass of water on his head.

LETTERS OF RECOMMENDATION

from Boothby the mixologist's earliest known employers.

From the Boothby scrapbook, courtesy of the California Historical Society.

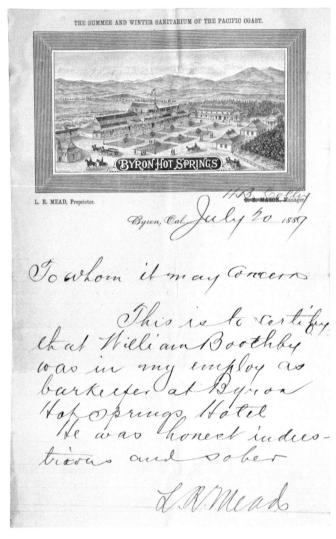

Byron, Cal., July 20, 1889

To whom it may concern

This is to certify that William Boothby was in my employ as barkeeper at Byron Hot Springs Hotel He was honest industrious and sober

L.R. Mead

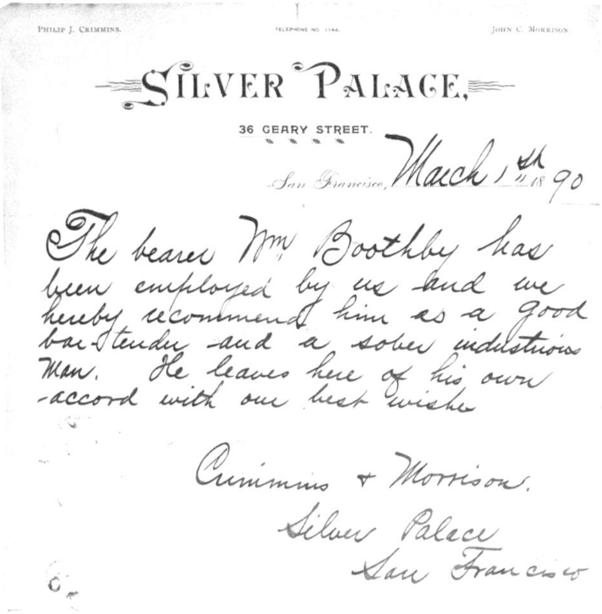

Philip J. Crimmins. Telephone No. 1144. John C. Morrison.

SILVER PALACE,

36 GEARY STREET.

San Francisco, March 1st 1890

The bearer Wm Boothby has been employed by us and we hereby recommend him as a good bar-tender and a sober industrious man. He leaves here of his own accord with our best wishes

Cummins & Morrison.
Silver Palace
San Francisco

San Francisco,
March 1, 1890

The bearer Wm. Boothby has been employed by us and we hereby recommend him as a good bar-tender and a sober industrious man. He leaves here of his own accord with our best wishes.

Cummins & Morrison.
Silver Palace
San Francisco

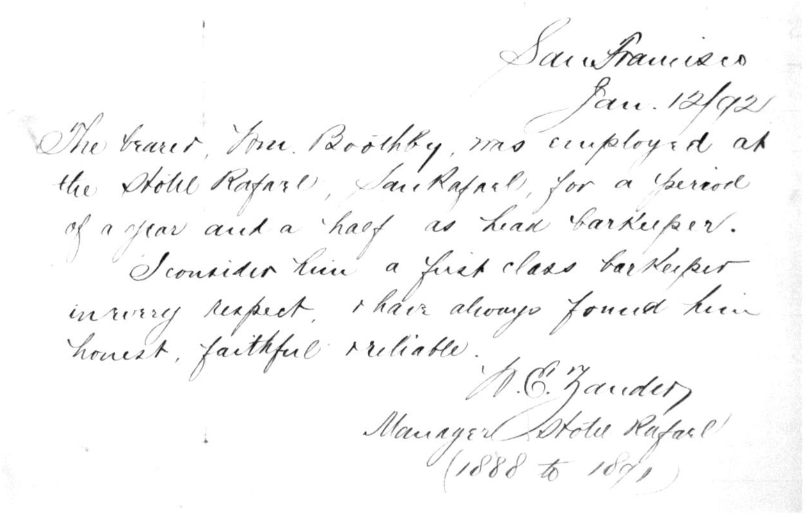

San Francisco
Jan. 12/92

The bearer, Wm. Boothby, was employed at the Hotel Rafael, San Rafael, for a period of a year and a half as head barkeeper.

I consider him a first class barkeeper in every respect, & have always found him honest, faithful & reliable.

W.E. Zander
Manager Hotel Rafael
(1888 to 1891)

San Francisco, Jan. 12, 1892

The bearer, Wm. Boothby, was employed at the Hotel Rafael, San Rafael, for a period of a year and a half as head barkeeper.

I consider him a first class barkeeper in every respect & have always found him honest, faithful & reliable.

W.E. Zander, Manager, Hotel Rafael (1888 to 1891)

Louis Roederer Champagne.

THE HIGHEST GRADE CHAMPAGNE IN THE WORLD.

CARTE BLANCHE		GRAND VIN SEC
(WHITE LABEL.)		(BROWN LABEL.)
A MAGNIFICENT RICH WINE.		PERFECTION OF A DRY WINE.

SEE THAT EVERY BOTTLE BEARS THE PRIVATE LABEL OF

MACONDRAY & CO.,

Sole Agents for the Pacific Coast.

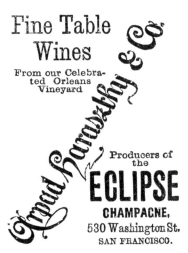

COCKTAIL BOOTHBY'S

AMERICAN BARTENDER

STANDARD | AUTHORITY.

THE ONLY PRACTICAL TREATISE ON THE ART OF MIXOLOGY PUBLISHED.

CONTAINING

Nearly Four Hundred Standard Recipes for the Mixing of Absinthes, Cocktails, Coolers, Cobblers, Crustas, Fixes, Flips, Fizzes, Hot Drinks, Lemonades, Punches, Sangarees, Shakes, Toddies, etc.;

ALSO

Much Valuable Information Relating to the Retail Liquor Business.

COPYRIGHT No. 31,866 V.

THE TRADE SUPPLIED BY THE SAN FRANCISCO NEWS COMPANY.

1891.

PRESS OF
H. S. CROCKER COMPANY,
SAN FRANCISCO.

INTRODUCTORY.

IN presenting this work to those desirous of becoming proficient in the bartender's art, I wish to thoroughly impress upon the minds of my readers that the recipes herein contained are considered standard in every sense of the word by all competent critics; therefore I willingly stake my well-earned reputation upon their practicability.

Many pamphlets heretofore written upon the theme of mixology are absolutely worthless, owing to the fact that they have been gotten up in the interest of some cheap publishing house which has paid some celebrated mixologist a royalty for the use of his name only, while some inexperienced, unprincipled individual is the real author. These so-called guides contain recipes for the mixing of beverages which no practical bartender on earth ever had occasion to serve. The only redeeming features of these decoctions are their high-sounding names, which scheming, imaginative penny-a-liners have given them in order to make large volumes out of little material.

I have neither asked nor received assistance of any description in the compilation of this book, the hints, suggestions, recipes and commandments being the fruit which my own individual tree of experience has borne. Therefore, I can challenge the world to ridicule or disprove anything herein contained.

Respectfully,

WM. T. (COCKTAIL) BOOTHBY,

Presiding Deity at the famous Hotel Rafael Club House,
SAN RAFAEL, CAL.

Late of the best houses in New York, Chicago, Philadelphia, New Orleans and Kansas City, and later of Byron Hot Springs, Cal., and the Silver Palace, San Francisco.

INDEX.

INDEX.

INDEX.

INDEX.

INDEX.

APPENDIX TO INDEX.

ABSINTHES

* * *

ABSINTHE COCKTAIL. 2.

(*See Receipe No. 16.*)

ABSINTHE FRAPPÉ OR FROZEN ABSINTHE. 3.

CALIFORNIA STYLE.

Into a medium-size mixing-glass of cracked ice pour a jigger of absinthe (if the customer desires sweetening add orgeat syrup to taste), fill the glass with water, shake until frost appears on the outside of the shaker, strain into thin cut glass and serve.

ABSINTHE FRAPPÉ OR FROZEN ABSINTHE. 4.

EASTERN STYLE.

Fill a medium-size mixing-glass with shaved ice; pour in a jigger of absinthe, shake until enough ice has dissolved to fill a small cut glass, strain and serve. No water or orgeat is used in this recipe; but, should a customer desire sweetening, a dash of orgeat may be added before shaking.

ABSINTHE PLAIN. 5.

FRENCH STYLE.

Pour a jigger of French absinthe into a thin glass; then fill an absinthe strainer (a glass or metallic vessel with a single hole in the center of the bottom) with cracked ice and water, and hold it high up over the glass containing the absinthe, allowing it to drip until the glass is full; then serve.

6.   ## ABSINTHE PLAIN.

A NICE WAY.

Fill a large bar strainer with fine ice, and set it on top of a medium-size cut glass with another glass alongside of it; now pour a jigger of absinthe over the ice (and a little orgeat if the customer desires it); and, when it is strained, place the strainer on the other glass, pour the contents of the first glass over the ice again, and continue to do this until enough ice has dissolved to fill one of the glasses; then serve.

7.   ## SUICESSE.

SAN FRANCISCO STYLE.

Into a medium-size mixing-glass place two or three lumps of ice, a dash of orgeat syrup and a jigger of absinthe. Shake until frost appears on the outside of shaker, strain into punch glass, fill up with cold syphon soda and serve.

8.

* ∴ *

9.   ## BRANDY COBBLER.

Dissolve a dessertspoonful of bar sugar in a little water in a medium-size mixing-glass, fill the glass with fine ice, add about a jigger and a half of cognac, shake thoroughly, decorate and serve with straws.

10.   ## CHAMPAGNE COBBLER.

Fill a cut-glass goblet with fine ice, and lay some assorted fruits on the top of it; then take a large mixing-glass and place in it one dessertspoonful of sugar and dissolve it in a little water; add a wineglassful of champagne (pour carefully), mix and then pour over the decorated ice in the goblet, and serve with straws.

CLARET COBBLER. 11.

Place a large spoonful of sugar in a large mixing-glass, fill the glass with fine ice and pour in all the claret the glass will hold. Shake thoroughly, decorate with fruits in season and serve with straws.

SHERRY COBBLER. 12.

Make the same as Claret Cobbler, with sherry wine substituted for claret.

WHISKEY COBBLER. 13.

Make the same as Brandy Cobbler, substituting the desired liquor for cognac.

WHITE WINE COBBLER. 14.

Make the same as Claret Cobbler, with the desired brand of white wine substituted for claret.

COCKTAILS 15.

ABSINTHE COCKTAIL. 16.

Fill a medium-size mixing-glass with fine ice, and pour over it five drops of Angostura, a dash of orgeat, a dash of anisette and about half a jigger of absinthe; stir well or shake, strain into small whiskey glass (cocktail glasses have gone out of date), add a piece of twisted lemon peel and serve.

BARRY COCKTAIL. 17.

Make the same as Martini Cocktail, with five drops of crème de mênthe added. (*See Receipe No. 27.*)

18.   BRANDY COCKTAIL.

In a small bar glass place one quarter of a teaspoonful of sugar with just enough water to dissolve it, a piece of ice about the size of an egg, three drops of Angostura bitters and a jigger of cognac; stir well until the beverage is well cooled, strain into small cut bar glass, throw in a piece of twisted lemon peel and serve with ice water on the side.

19.   CHAMPAGNE COCKTAIL.

Place in a champagne glass two or three lumps of ice, on the top of which lay a cube of sugar with a pair of sugar tongs. Saturate the sugar with Angostura bitters, fill the glass with champagne (the desired brand), stir carefully and serve.

If the wine is cold omit the ice, as ice impairs the flavor of wine.

Some bartenders decorate this drink with fruits, but that is a matter of taste.

20.   DUDE COCKTAIL.

Into a large bar glass place two or three lumps of ice and a pony of crème de vanille; fill the glass with lemon soda or sweet soda and a little lime juice, stir, decorate with fruits and serve with straws. Keep the doors closed so the draughts will not affect the creature.

21.   DUTCH COCKTAIL.

A glass of beer.

22.   FANCY WHISKEY COCKTAIL.

Dissolve one-quarter of a teaspoonful of bar sugar in a dessertspoonful of water in a small mixing-glass; add a piece of ice, a dash of Curaçoa, three drops of Angostura bitters, a jigger of whiskey and a piece of twisted lemon peel; stir thoroughly, strain into a frosted glass and serve with ice water on the side.

23.   GIN COCKTAIL.

Into a small mixing-glass place a piece of ice, a dash of gum syrup, a long dash of Bonnekamp bitters and about ten drops of orange bitters or two drops of Selner bitters; twist and throw in a small piece of lemon peel and add a jigger of Holland gin. This drink to be palatable must be served very cold; therefore a thorough stirring is necessary.

JAPANESE COCKTAIL. 24.

Make the same as a Brandy Cocktail, substituting orgeat syrup in place of a little sugar and water.

JERSEY COCKTAIL. 25.

Fill a large bar glass with cracked ice, and add a spoonful of sugar and a dash of Angostura bitters; flavor with apple jack, fill up with good cider, throw in a piece of twisted lemon peel, stir and serve.

MANHATTAN COCKTAIL. 26.

Into a small mixing-glass place one-quarter teaspoonful of sugar, two teaspoonfuls of water, three drops of Angostura, one-half jiggerful of whiskey, and one-half jiggerful of vermouth; stir, strain into a small bar glass, twist lemon peel and throw in and serve with ice water on the side.

MARTINI COCKTAIL. 27.

This popular appetizer is made without sweetening of any description, as the Old Tom Cordial gin and the Italian vermouth of which it is composed are both sweet enough. Into a small mixing-glass place a piece of ice, four drops of Angostura bitters, half a jigger of Old Tom Cordial gin, half a jigger of Italian vermouth and a piece of twisted lemon peel; stir thoroughly, strain into a small bar glass and serve with ice water.

MIKADO COCKTAIL. 28.

Another name for a Japanese Cocktail. (*See Receipe No. 24.*)

OLD TOM GIN COCKTAIL. 29.

Make the same as Holland Gin Cocktail, with Old Tom gin substituted for Holland gin. (*See Receipe No. 23.*)

OLD TOM GIN (CORDIAL) COCKTAIL. 30.

Never use sweetening of any description in this drink, as the cordial gin is sweet enough. Into a small mixing-glass place a piece of ice, about a teaspoonful of orange bitters, a jigger of Old Tom Cordial and a piece of twisted lemon peel; stir, strain into a small bar glass and serve with ice water on the side.

31.   **PINEAPPLE COCKTAIL.**

Into a small mixing-glass place two teaspoonfuls of pineapple syrup, three drops of Angostura bitters, a piece of ice and a jigger of the desired liquor ; stir thoroughly, strain into small bar glass, add a small slice of pineapple and serve with ice water on the side.

32.   **RUM COCKTAIL.**

Make the same as Brandy Cocktail, with Jamaica rum substituted for brandy.

33.   **SODA COCKTAIL.**

Place two or three lumps of ice in a large bar glass with a teaspoonful of bar sugar and two dashes or Angostura bitters. Fill the glass with lemon soda or sweet soda and a little lime juice, stir briskly and serve immediately.

34.   **TURF COCKTAIL.**

Into a small mixing-glass dissolve one-quarter teaspoonful of bar sugar in a teaspoonful of water. Add a piece of ice, three drops of Angostura bitters, half a jiggerful of Holland gin and half a jiggerful of vermouth. Stir thoroughly, add a piece of twisted lemon peel, strain into small bar glass and serve with ice water on the side. A small dash of orange bitters may be added to this drink.

35.   **VERMOUTH COCKTAIL.**

Make the same as a Brandy Cocktail, with either French or Italian vermouth substituted for brandy.

36.   **WHISKEY COCKTAIL.**

Make the same as Brandy Cocktail, with whiskey substituted for cognac.

♣ CRUSTAS ♣ 37.

BRANDY CRUSTA. 38.

Prepare a stem claret glass by rubbing the rim with a piece of lemon. Then dip the edge in bar sugar so as to frost the glass. Pare a lemon as you would an apple, so the peel will all be in one piece; lay the peel in the glass carefully with a fork or sugar tongs, so it will just fit the interior of the glass. Now take a medium-size mixing-glass three-quarters full of cracked ice, and add four drops of Angostura bitters, one dash of gum and a taste of maraschino. Throw in a jigger of good cognac and a few drops of lime juice, stir thoroughly, strain into prepared glass, decorate and serve.

GIN CRUSTA. 39.

This drink is made like a Brandy Crusta, with Holland gin substituted for cognac and two dashes of Bonnekamp bitters used in place of four drops of Angostura bitters.

WHISKEY CRUSTA. 40.

The same as Brandy Crusta, with bourbon whiskey substituted for cognac.

DAISIES 41.

BRANDY DAISY. 42.

Half fill a medium-size mixing-glass with cracked ice, add the juice of one lime, three dashes of orange cordial and a jigger of brandy. Shake, strain into a punch glass, fill up with syphon seltzer and serve.

43.   **WHISKEY, GIN AND RUM DAISIES.**

All made the same as the preceding recipe, with the desired brand of liquor substituted for cognac.

44.   **✦ FIXES ✦**

45.   **BRANDY FIX.**

Fill a punch glass with fine ice and set it on the bar. Then take a medium-size mixing-glass and put in it one dessertspoonful of sugar, the juice of one lemon, a jigger of whiskey and enough water to make a drink large enough to fill the punch glass containing the ice. Stir well, pour over the ice in the punch glass, decorate and serve with straws.

46.   **GIN FIX.**

Make the same as preceding recipe, substituting Holland gin for brandy.

47.   **RUM FIX.**

Make the same as Brandy Fix, substituting Jamaica rum for brandy.

48.   **SHERRY FIX.**

Make the same as Brandy Fix, substituting sherry for brandy.

49.   **WHISKEY FIX.**

Make the same as Brandy Fix, substituting whiskey for brandy.

FIZZES

GIN FIZZ, PLAIN. 51.

Place a dessertspoonful of sugar in a small mixing-glass with the juice of one lemon. Add a jigger of Holland gin and two lumps of ice. Shake thoroughly, strain into thin glass, fill with syphon seltzer off the ice and serve immediately.

GINGER ALE FIZZ. 52.

Make the same as Plain Gin Fizz, substituting ginger ale in place of syphon seltzer.

GOLDEN FIZZ. 53.

Add the yolk of an egg to a Plain Gin Fizz and shake thoroughly.

MORNING GLORY FIZZ. 54.

Place a dessertspoonful of sugar and the juice of one lemon in a medium-size mixing-glass, add two dashes of absinthe previously dissolved in a little water, the white of one egg and a jigger of either gin or whiskey (whichever the customer prefers). Place a few lumps of ice in a shaker and shake well, strain into large punch glass, fill with syphon seltzer and serve immediately.

OLD TOM GIN FIZZ. 55.

Made the same as Plain Gin Fizz, with Old Tom gin substituted for Holland gin. In using Old Tom Cordial always use a little less sugar, as the cordial is much sweeter than plain gin.

ROYAL FIZZ. 56.

This is an Old Tom Gin Fizz with a pony of crême de vanille added.

SILVER FIZZ. 57.

Make the same as Plain Gin Fizz with the white of an egg added. Shake well.

58. # FLIPS

59. ### BRANDY FLIP.

Place a dessertspoonful of sugar in a medium-size mixer, break an egg in a clean glass to ascertain that it is fresh, and then throw it in. Add a few lumps of ice and a jigger of cognac, shake thoroughly, strain into small cut class, grate nutmeg on top and serve.

60. ### GIN FLIP.

Make the same as Brandy Flip, with Holland gin substituted for brandy.

61. ### SHERRY FLIP.

Make the same as Brandy Flip, with sherry wine substituted for brandy.

62. ### WHISKEY FLIP.

Make the same as Brandy Flip, with whiskey substituted for brandy.

63.

64. ### ABSINTHE FRAPPÉ.

(*See Recipes Nos. 3 and 4.*)

CHAMPAGNE FRAPPÉ. 65.

Place the bottle of wine which you desire to cool in a champagne cooler or ice-cream freezer, and pack the space between the inner and outer vessels with two parts ice and one part salt. If no cooler or freezer is available, wrap the bottle in a towel, place it in a bucket and pack the space around the bottle with salt and ice. Cover with a napkin to keep the cold air in, and the longer it stands the colder it will get.

CRÊME DE MÊNTHE FRAPPÉ. 66.

Fill a small cut glass with shaved or fine cracked ice, and pour as much crême de mênthe over it as the glass will hold. This is a most popular after-dinner beverage with the upper ten.

FRAPPÉ DRINKS. 67.

Frappé is a French word meaning frozen; therefore a frappé drink is a frozen one, or any liqueur or other beverage poured over and served with fine ice is considered à la frappé.

VERMOUTH FRAPPÉ. 68.

Fill a medium-size mixing-glass with fine ice, and pour over it one and one-half jiggers of either French or Italian vermouth, shake thoroughly, strain into small cut bar glass and serve.

HOT DRINKS 69.

ALE HOT OR MULLED ALE. 70.

Place an iron which has been heated to a white heat in a pewter mug of ale. Immerse slowly, being careful not to allow the ale to run over the sides of the mug, and serve.

71. ## ALE SANGAREE, HOT.

Dissolve a spoonful of bar sugar in a little hot water in a mug, fill the mug with ale, immerse a white-hot iron into the ale until the desired temperature has been attained, grate nutmeg over the top and serve.

72. ## ALHAMBRA ROYAL.

Pour a pony of cognac into a cup of chocolate and add a little lime juice to it.

73. ## APPLE BRANDY, HOT.

Fill a hot-water glass three quarters full of boiling water and dissolve in it a cube of sugar. Add as much apple brandy as the glass will hold, stir, spice to taste and serve.

74. ## BEEF TEA.

Dissolve a teaspoonful of Liston's or Leibig's extract of beef in a cup, mug or glass of boiling water, season to taste with celery salt and pepper, and serve. Maggi's Bouillon and Armer's Vigoral are also highly recommended.

75. ## BLACK STRIPE, HOT.

Into a hot-water glass place a teaspoonful of molasses and fill the glass two-thirds full of boiling water. Dissolve the molasses and fill the glass with St. Croix rum and serve after stirring. A little spice of any description can be served with this drink.

76. ## BLUE BLAZER.

Use two mugs. Dissolve a teaspoonful of sugar in a little hot water in one mug, and place a wineglassful of Scotch whiskey in the other one. Set the liquor afire and pour the burning liquor from one mug to another until the desired temperature has been attained, throw in a piece of twisted lemon peel for a flavor and serve.

77. ## BRANDY BURNT.

Place two lumps of sugar in a saucer and pour over them a jigger of brandy. Set the liquor afire and let it burn until all the sugar is dissolved, mixing and stirring the while. Serve in hot-water glass.

BRANDY BURNT AND PEACH. 78.

FOR DIARRHŒA.

Place two or three slices of dried peaches in a hot-water glass and pour burnt brandy made according to the preceding recipe over them. Serve with nutmeg.

BRANDY FLIP, HOT. 79.

A Hot Brandy Toddy with a piece of roasted cracker on top is a Hot Brandy Flip.

BRANDY SLING, HOT. 80.

Place a cube of sugar in a hot-water glass, fill the glass two-thirds full of boiling water, dissolve the sugar, fill the glass with cognac and serve with grated nutmeg.

BRANDY TODDY, HOT. 81.

Dissolve a cube of sugar in a hot-water glass two-thirds full of boiling water, fill the glass with cognac, add a slice of lemon and serve.

BUTTERED RUM, HOT. 82.

Make the same as a Hot Rum Sling with a teaspoonful of butter added.

CAFÉ ROYAL. 83.

Hold over a cup of good, hot, black coffee a teaspoon containing a lump of sugar saturated with yellow Chartreuse and set on fire, allowing it to burn until the sugar is dissolved. Mix well and serve.

CLARET, HOT. 84.

FOR ONE PERSON.

Dissolve two cubes of sugar in a hot-water glass half full of boiling water, fill the glass with claret, add a slice of lemon, grate nutmeg over the top and serve.

85.   CRANBERRYADE.

Place about a dozen cranberries in a large mixing-glass and mash them well with a muddler. Add some boiling water, strain into thin glass, sweeten to taste, dash with port wine and serve. Any kind of berries can be treated in the same manner.

86.   EGG FLIP, HOT.

Pour a pint of Bass' ale in a saucepan and set on the fire to boil. Then beat up a couple of eggs and mix with two tablespoonfuls of sugar (brown sugar is the best), making a light batter. When the ale has boiled, pour over the eggs very slowly at first to prevent curdling, then pour backwards and forwards until the mixture appears all alike and smooth. Spice well and serve as hot as possible. This is an old English cure for a bad cold.

87.   EGG NOG, HOT.

Make the same as Cold Egg Nog, with hot milk substituted for ice and milk. (*See Recipes Nos. 163 and 164.*)

88.   GIN SLING, HOT.

Make the same as Brandy Sling, Hot, with Holland gin substituted for brandy. (*See Recipe No. 80.*)

89.   GIN TODDY, HOT.

Make the same as Brandy Toddy, Hot, with Holland gin substituted for brandy. (*See Recipe No. 81.*)

90.   IRISH WHISKEY, HOT.

Place a cube of sugar in a small hot-water glass, fill the glass three-quarters full of boiling water, stir until sugar is dissolved, fill the glass with good Irish whiskey, add a small slice of lemon, spice to taste and serve.

91.   LEMONADE, HOT.

Place two cubes of sugar and the juice of one lemon in a thin glass, fill with hot water, stir until sugar is dissolved, add a slice of lemon and serve.

LOCOMOTIVE. 92.

Into a large mixing-glass place a tablespoonful of sugar, a teaspoonful of honey, a pony of Curaçoa, the yolk of one egg and a claret glass of claret. Mix well and boil in a saucepan. Take another saucepan and pour the drink from one pan to the other uutil the mixture attains a smooth appearance. Pour into a large mug, grate nutmeg over top, add a slice of lemon and serve.

MILK PUNCH, HOT. 93.

Make the same as Cold Milk Punch with hot milk substituted for cold milk and ice. (*See Recipe No. 236.*)

MONKEY PUNCH, HOT. 94.

A SOUTHERN WINTER DRINK.

Dissolve a teaspoonful of sugar in a hot-water glass half full of boiling water. Fill the glass with St. Julien wine, add a slice of lemon, grate nutmeg over top and serve.

MULLED OR HOT WINE. 95.

Dissolve six large spoonfuls of sugar and the juice of six lemons in half a pint of boiling water. Heat a bottle of the desired brand of wine to a boiling point in a clean metallic vessel, and add the flavored water to it. Spice well with nutmeg, add a sprig of mint or verbena, and serve in thin glassware.

MULLED OR HOT WINE WITH EGGS. 96.

A SIMPLE RECIPE FOR ANY WINE.

Dissolve one-quarter pound of sugar in one pint of boiling water, add the juice of six lemons and one and one-half bottles of the desired wine. Keep over the fire until just ready to boil. In the interim beat up the whites of one dozen eggs until they appear like froth, and place them in a punch bowl which has been heated. Then pour in the hot mixture (stirring rapidly to prevent the eggs from cooking), spice well and serve in thin glassware.

N. B.—Don't pour the eggs into the wine.

PORTER MULLED, OR HOT PORTER. 97.

The same as mulled ale, with Dublin stout substituted for ale. (*See Recipe No. 70.*)

98. **PORTER SANGAREE, HOT.**

Make the same as Ale Sangaree, Hot, substituting Dublin stout for ale. (*See Recipe No. 71.*)

99. **PORT WINE NEGUS, HOT.**

Dissolve a teaspoonful of bar sugar in a hot-water glass three-quarters full of boiling water. Fill the glass with port wine, stir, and serve without decorations, flavors or spices of any description.

100. **PORT WINE SANGAREE, HOT.**

Place a spoonful of sugar in a hot-water glass and fill two-thirds full of boiling water. Stir until sugar is dissolved and add enough port wine to fill the glass, grate nutmeg over the top and serve.

101. **ROYAL PUNCH, HOT.**

Place two tablespoonfuls of sugar and the juice of four lemons in a small punch bowl and dissolve in one pint of boiling tea. Add half a pint of cognac, a jigger of Curaçoa and the well-beaten whites of three eggs. Serve as hot as possible in thin glassware.

102. **RUM SLING, HOT.**

Make the same as Hot Brandy Sling, with Jamacia rum substituted for cognac. (*See Recipe No. 80.*)

103. **RUM TODDY, HOT.**

Make the same as Hot Brandy Toddy, with Jamaica rum substituted for cognac. (*See Recipe No. 81*).

104. **SCOTCH, HOT.**

Dissolve a cube of sugar in a hot-water glass three-quarters full of boiling water, add enough Scotch whiskey to nearly fill the glass, throw in a piece of lemon peel and a clove, and grate nutmeg over the top.

SPICED RUM, HOT.   105.

Dissolve a cube of sugar in a hot-water glass three-quarters full of boiling water, add enough Jamaica rum to nearly fill the glass, put in some assorted spices and serve.

N. B.— A small piece of butter may be added to this drink with the customer's permission.

TAM O'SHANTER.   106.

This drink is made the same as Hot Whiskey Punch, with old Islay whiskey substituted for bourbon whiskey. (*See Recipe No. 110.*)

TEA PUNCH, HOT.   107.

Make a quart of good, well-steeped tea. Then take a large punch bowl and put in three-quarters of a pint of cognac, one-quarter of a pint of Jamaica rum, the fresh juice of four lemons and six heaping tablespoonfuls of sugar. Set this mixture on fire and stir rapidly, adding the hot tea slowly the while. A nice way of flavoring this drink is to mash the rinds of the lemons into the sugar with a muddler before placing the sugar in the bowl. When the sugar has absorbed all the moisture from the rinds, throw them away.

TOM AND JERRY.   108.

To make this celebrated beverage, a batter must first be prepared in the following manner. Procure any number of eggs and separate the whites from the yolks. Beat the whites until stiff and the yolks until thin ; then pour both together into a large bowl and mix with enough sugar to make a thick paste. Your batter is now ready, so when you wish to make a Tom and Jerry, rinse out a mug, cup or glass with boiling water (this is done to heat it), place a heaping teaspoonful of the batter into the hot mug (mugs are generally used to serve this drink), add a jigger of cognac and a dash of St. Croix rum, fill the glass with hot milk (some use hot water), and stir until the batter is all dissolved, grate nutmeg on top and serve.

N. B.—A half teaspoonful of carbonate of soda stirred into Tom and Jerry batter will keep it sweet and prevent the sugar from settling to the bottom of the bowl.

WATER, HOT.   109.

Place a spoon in a hot-water glass full of boiling water and serve. Dyspeptics claim this as a great relief for their affliction.

110. ### WHISKEY PUNCH, HOT.

Dissolve a cube of sugar in a hot-water glass two-thirds full of boiling water, pour in enough of the desired brand of whiskey to nearly fill the glass and add a few drops of lemon juice, a slice of lemon and some spice.

111. ### WHISKEY SLING, HOT.

Make the same as Brandy Sling, Hot, substituting the desired brand of whiskey for cognac. (*See Recipe No. 80.*)

112. ### WHISKEY TODDY, HOT.

Make the same as Hot Brandy Toddy, substituting the desired brand of whiskey for cognac. (*See Recipe No. 81.*)

113. ### YARD OF FLANNEL.

ENGLISH.

Make the same as Hot Egg Flip. (*See Recipe No. 86.*)

114.

115. ### BRANDY JULEP.

THE NEW STYLE.

Fill a large goblet with fine ice and pour a jigger of cognac over it; then take several sprigs of young, tender mint and place them in a medium-size mixing-glass with a dessertspoonful of bar sugar and just enough water to nearly fill the goblet, in which you have already placed the fine ice and brandy. Press the mint with a muddler until the sugar is all dissolved and the water is well flavored with mint, strain into the goblet of ice and brandy, dash with Jamaica rum, ornament with fruits and a few sprigs of mint which have been moistened and dipped in sugar, and serve with straws.

GIN JULEP. 116.

Make the same as Brandy Julep, with Holland gin substituted for brandy and the rum flavor omitted.

MINT JULEP. 117.

The same as Brandy Julep.

RUM JULEP. 118.

Make the same as Brandy Julep, with Jamaica rum substituted for cognac.

WHISKEY JULEP. 119.

Make the same as Brandy Julep, with whiskey substituted for cognac.

LEMONADES 120.

APOLLINARIS LEMONADE. 121.

Place a piece of ice in a large goblet and set the glass on the bar in front of the customer. Then place a tablespoonful of sugar and the juice of two limes in a large mixing-glass with just enough Apollinaris to dissolve the sugar. Stir well until sugar is dissolved, pour into the prepared goblet; then fill the goblet with Apollinaris, decorate and serve with straws.

CENTENNIAL LEMONADE. 122.

Into a large mixing-glass place a tablespoonful of sugar, the juice of two limes, the white of an egg and some cracked ice. Fill the glass with water, shake thoroughly, strain into a cut goblet, decorate and serve with straws.

123.   **CIRCUS LEMONADE.**

This drink in a bar-room is a Plain Lemonade colored with raspberry sprup; but a Circus Lemonade proper is a beverage that is sold on race courses and fair grounds, and is made in the following manner:

Procure a large tub or headless barrel and fill it nearly full of water; add enough tartaric acid to suit and sweeten to taste with sugar (two pounds of tartaric acid will make over thirty gallons of lemonade). Red aniline is used for coloring. Always slice up a few lemons, limes or oranges and throw in. If you have no ice handy with which to cool this delightful beverage, procure a piece of glass and fasten it to the sides of the barrel with strings so it will float near the top, and put some of the sliced fruit on it. This little deception causes the drink to appear more inviting on a warm day.

124.   **CLARET LEMONADE.**

A Plain Lemonade dashed with claret.

125.   **EGG LEMONADE.**

Into a large mixing-glass place a tablespoonful of sugar, the juice of two limes, a fresh raw egg and some cracked ice. Fill the glass with water, shake thoroughly, strain into large cut goblet, decorate and serve with straws.

126.   **LEMON SQUASH.**

The British name for a Plain Lemonade.

127.   **NAPA SODA LEMONADE.**

Make the same as Apollinaris Lemonade, with Napa soda water substituted for Apollinaris.

128.   **ORGEAT LEMONADE.**

A sour Plain Lemonade dashed with orgeat syrup.

129.   **PLAIN LEMONADE.**

Into a large mixing-glass place a tablespoonful of bar sugar, the juice of two limes and just enough water to dissolve the sugar, stir thoroughly and pour into a large goblet containing a piece of ice, fill the goblet with water, stir, decorate and serve with straws.

PORT WINE LEMONADE. 130.

A Plain Lemonade dashed with port.

RASPBERRY LEMONADE. 131.

A Plain Lemonade colored with raspberry syrup.

SELTZER LEMONADE. 132.

Make the same as Plain Lemonade, with seltzer water substituted for plain water.

SHERRY LEMONADE. 133.

A Plain Lemonade dashed with sherry wine.

SODA LEMONADE. 134.

Make the same as Plain Lemonade, with syphon or plain soda substituted for water.

SPIKE LEMONADE. 135.

A Plain Lemonade dashed with whiskey.

TEXAS LEMONADE. 136.

Another name for Spike Lemonade. Sometimes spoken of as a lemonade with a wink, or a lemonade with a stick in it.

137.

Miscellaneous Drinks

138. AMER PICON.

A POPULAR FRENCH BEVERAGE.

Into a medium-size cut glass place a piece of ice, a jigger of amer picon and a pony of orgeat or gum syrup. Fill the glass with syphon seltzer and serve.

139. ARCHBISHOP.

Into a medium-size mixing-glass place a spoonful of sugar dissolved in a jigger of water; add a little cracked ice and a jigger of port wine. Shake thoroughly, pour into a punch glass, add a slice of lemon, dash with Jamaica rum and serve with straws.

140. 'ARF AND 'ARF, OR BLACK AND TAN.

ENGLISH.

A mug or glass containing half porter and half ale. (*See Half and Half Recipe No. 173.*)

141. "AULD MAN'S MILK."

SCOTCH.

Another name for Egg Nogg. (*See Recipes Nos. 163 and 164.*)

142. B. AND S.

The English way of ordering a Brandy and Soda. (*See Recipe No. 149.*)

BALTIMORE KISSES.   143.

Sweeten the well-beaten whites of four eggs to taste with maple sugar and place in a small punch bowl with a half bottle of currant wine off the ice. Serve in thin glassware for two. A larger quantity can be made by using the above recipe for proportion.

BISHOP.   144.

Make a lemonade of any effervescent water, to which add a jigger of Burgundy and a dash of Jamaica rum. Stir, decorate and serve with straws.

BLACK STRIPE, COLD.   145.

FOR SORE THROAT.

Place a teaspoonful of molasses in a small bar glass with a jigger of St. Croix rum. Stir well and serve.

BONANZA.   146.

Into a stem claret glass place a piece of ice, a pony of brandy and a jigger and a half of angelica. Fill the balance with reisling, stir and serve.

BRANDY CHAMPERELLE.   147.

Place equal quantities of crème de cassis, maraschino, yellow Chartreuse and cognac in a sherry glass in the order named, not allowing the ingredients to mix. Serve with ice water.

BRANDY AND GUM.   148.

Place about a teaspoonful of gum syrup in a small bar glass containing a small teaspoon. Set in front of customer with a bottle of cognac at his right hand and serve water on the side after stirring.

BRANDY AND SODA.   149.

Place a medium-size bar glass in front of the customer with a bottle or decanter of cognac at his right, allowing him to help himself to the liquor; then fill the glass with cold syphon soda and serve.

150.   **BRECK AND BRACE.**

A '49ERS BEVERAGE.

Fill a small bar glass with water and throw it out again, then fill the glass with bar sugar and throw that out, leaving the glass apparently frosted inside. pour in a jigger of cognac and fill the glass with cold champagne. Then smile.

151.   **CARDINAL FOR A PARTY.**

Dissolve six tablespoonfuls of sugar in the juice of ten lemons and one bottle of plain soda. Add a jigger of yellow Chartreuse and pour in a large bottle of Burgundy and a pint of Sauterne. Mix thoroughly, place a large piece of ice in the bowl, decorate with slices of orange and pineapple and a few sprigs of mint, and serve in thin glassware.

152.   **CHAMPAGNE CUP.**

See Claret and Champagne Cup (*Recipe No. 156*).

153.   **CHAMPERELLE.**

Another name for Pousse Café. See Brandy Champerelle (*Recipe No. 147*), and Pousse Café (*Recipe No. 189*).

154.   **CHASER.**

A small glass of malt liquor served on the side with any spirituous liquor is called a Chaser.

155.   **CIDER NECTAR.**

Fill a punch glass with fine ice and set it in front of the customer. Then take a large mixing-glass and put in it a dessertspoonful of sugar, the juice of two limes, a dash of whiskey or brandy and some cider. Stir until sugar is dissolved and then pour over the fine ice in the punch glass, decorate with fruits in season and serve with straws.

CLARET AND CHAMPAGNE CUP. 156.

For one quart of claret take the juice of four peeled lemons and two oranges which have been squeezed into a bowl containing four tablespoonfuls of bar sugar; in this bowl now macerate the leaves of six sprigs of mint; then pour in one pony of Jamaica rum, two ponies of brandy and two of maraschino or some other cordial; stir the whole like wildfire and then pour in the claret; to the whole then add one bottle of plain soda (or one of champagne if Champagne Cup be desired) one pint of Rhine wine and the peel of a cucumber; cut up one small pineapple or take a can of preserved pineapples and some sliced seedless oranges to garnish the whole, and pour into a bowl around one large lump of ice and serve in thin glassware.

CLARET AND SELTZER. 157.

Place a piece of ice in a long thin glass and fill with half claret and half syphon seltzer.

COLLINS. 158.

There are many kinds of Collins, viz., John Collins, which is made with Holland gin; Tom Collins with Tom gin; Whiskey Collins with the liquor designated etc., etc. A Collins, however, is nothing more or less than a fizz; but it is usually made as a very long drink. See Fizzes (*Recipe No. 50*), and John Collins (*Recipe No. 177*).

COOLERS. 159.

There are two popular drinks called coolers which have no other distinguishable title. One is made by mixing equal parts of milk and seltzer; and the other is simply a ginger ale lemonade or a lemonade made of ginger ale instead of water. It is customary for barkeepers to ask a customer which he prefers.

N. B.—Some years ago, the late William Remsen, a retired naval officer and a popular member of the Union Club, N. Y., introduced a beverage to the members of that swell organization which has since taken his name and is now known to all clubmen by the appellation of Remsen cooler. The following recipe is the correct thing and has never before appeared in print. Pare a lemon (a lime will not answer the purpose) as you would an apple, so the peel will resemble a corkscrew, place the rind in a long thin glass and pour over it a full jigger of Old Tom Cordial gin; with a bar-spoon now press the peel and stir it thouroughly so the liquor will be well flavored with the essence of the skin and fill the glass with plain soda off the ice. English soda is highly recommended for this drink.

160.   COPENHAGEN.

Place a teaspoonful of Tom and Jerry batter (*See Recipe No. 108*) in a mug or glass, add a dash of rum, fill with lemon soda, stir until dissolved and serve.

161.   DELIGHTS.

A delight is a mixture of equal parts of French ratafia and cognac served in a pony glass with ice water on the side.

N. B.—There are many delights which have been named after their originators; as Jake Sharpe's delight, Wintgen's delight, etc. But these beverages are only known to a few patrons of the houses which have tried in vain to popularize them. As this work contains only standard recipes, I do not feel justified in publishing directions for the compounding of drinks which possess only local reputations.

THE AUTHOR.

162.   DOG'S NOSE.

ENGLISH.

A mug or glass of porter dashed with Old Tom Cordial gin has been termed a Dog's Nose.

163.   EGG NOG.

Place a dessertspoonful of bar sugar in a large mixing-glass; add some fine ice, a raw egg, a jigger of cognac and a dash of St. Croix rum. Fill the glass with good milk, shake thoroughly, grate nutmeg over the top and serve with straws.

164.   EGG NOG.

ONE GALLON.

Dissolve eight tablespoonfuls of sugar in three quarts of milk in a punch bowl, to which add three-quarters of a bottle of cognac and one-quarter of a bottle of St. Croix rum; now beat the yolks of ten eggs until thin, and the whites until frothy; stir the yolks into the above mixture and lay the beaten whites carefully over the top. Sprinkle with nutmeg and serve as cold as possible without ice.

N. B.—By filling a syphon soda bottle with some of the above mixture and addding a cake of compressed yeast to it, an effervescent draught fit for the gods can be produced. After filling the bottle and adding the yeast, put it in a warm place for five or six hours and then remove it to a cool place for a few days before using, when enough gas will have generated in the bottle to cause it to flow like soda. This is a splendid thing for invalids.

EGG NOG, SHERRY. 165.

Substitute sherry for cognac and St. Croix rum, and follow the directions in the two preceding recipes.

GIN AND BITTERS. 166.

Rinse the interior of a small bar glass with a dash of the desired brand of bitters (Bonnekamp is generally used with gin), hand the customer a bottle of Holland gin, allow him to help himself and serve ice water on the side.

GIN AND GUM. 167.

Place a little gum syrup in a small bar glass, hand the gin bottle and glass with a spoon to the customer, and serve ice water on the side.

GIN AND PINE. 168.

Into a decanter of good Holland gin place several splinters from a piece of green pine wood. When this drink is ordered, place the decanter at the customer's right and hand him a small bar glass containing a small piece of ice, allowing the gentleman to help himself. Always serve ice water on the side. Whiskey and brandy are also used with pine.

GIN AND SODA. 169.

Hand a long thin glass to the customer with the gin bottle at his right. After he has helped himself, fill the glass with cold syphon soda.

GIN AND TANSY. 170.

Fill a decanter with tansy leaves and cover them with good Holland gin. In a few days it will be ready to serve. When the bottle is empty refill with gin, and continue to do so until all the strength of the leaves has departed. Serve plain with water on the side.

GIN AND WORMWOOD. 171.

Made the same as Gin and Tansy with wormwood substituted for tansy.

172.   GOLDEN SLIPPER.

Half fill a sherry glass with yellow Chartreuse, on the top of which place the yolk of an egg and fill the glass with goldwasser.

173.   HALF AND HALF.

A glass or mug containing half porter and half ale.

174.   HONEY AND PEACH.

Place a teaspoonful of strained honey in a small bar glass, hand the customer the decanter of peach brandy, and, when he has helped himself, stir until the honey is dissolved and serve ice water on the side.

175.   ICEBERG.

Fill a large mixing-glass with fine ice and add the juice of one lemon, a jigger of raspberry syrup and a jigger of California rum. Stir until enough ice dissolves to fill an ordinary punch glass, into which you then strain it, and after adding a little fruit serve with straws.

176.   IRISH HALF AND HALF.

Half fill a large bar glass with whiskey, then fill the other half with whiskey (any kind of whiskey will do), hand the customer a bath tub, towels and soap and charge wholesale rates.

177.   JOHN COLLINS.

Take the largest glass procurable and place a good size piece of ice in it. Set this in front of the customer with a bottle of Holland gin at his right hand so he can serve himself to the gin. Then take a large mixing-glass and put in it the juice of two lemons, a heaping tablespoonful of bar sugar, and dissolve this in part of a bottle of plain soda; pour into the large glass of gin and ice, fill up the glass with the balance of the plain soda, stir and serve. Many bartenders make a regular Gin Fizz and serve it for a John Collins; but this recipe is standard and is highly recommended as a morning bracer after a night of dissipation.

KNICKEBEIN. 178.

Break an egg carefully so as not to fracture the tender covering of the yolk. Place the white in a bowl or mixing-glass and softly lay the yolk in the bottom of a very small claret glass. Now nearly fill the glass containing the yolk with equal parts of benedictine, yellow Chartreuse, kummel and cognac (crême de vanille is sometimes added). No caution need be used to prevent the ingredients from mixing as in a pousse café; and the yolk of the egg must not be placed in the glass after any liqueur, as it should lay on the bottom. After these preparations have been completed, beat the white of the egg which you have in the bowl or mixing-glass until it becomes stiff, sweeten to taste with bar sugar and with a teaspoon place a heavy layer over the decoction which you have just prepared. Dash with Angostura bitters, sprinkle with a little ground cinnamon and serve.

KNICKEBEIN. 179.

DIRECTIONS FOR TAKING.

This celebrated Teutonic decoction is little known in America, and few bartenders have ever acquired the art of compounding one. It is an after-dinner drink, and, in order to be fully appreciated, it must be partaken of according to the following directions. Should the drinker not abide by these rules, the desired effect of the beverage will not be experienced. Therefore, the duty of the presiding mixologist is to thoroughly explain to the uninitiated the *modus operandi,* etc.

1. Pass the glass under the nose and inhale the flavor for about five seconds.

2. Hold the glass perpendicularly, open your mouth wide and suck the froth from off the top of the glass. Pause five seconds.

3. Point the lips and take one-third of the liquid contents of the glass without touching the yolk. Pause again for a few seconds.

4. Straighten the body, throw the head back, swallow the contents remaining in the glass and break the yolk in your mouth at the same time.

LA CREOLE. 180.

A RAINBOW POUSSE CAFÉ WITHOUT COGNAC.

Pour carefully into a sherry glass, so the colors will not mix, equal parts of the following ingredients in the order named: Raspberry syrup, maraschino, yellow Chartreuse and green Chartreuse. This beverage is very popular with the fair sex in some parts of the Southern states and West Indies.

181.   LAWN TENNIS COOLER.

A NEW AND POPULAR BEVERAGE.

Into a medium-size mixing-glass, place a tablespoonful of sugar, the juice of two limes, one raw egg and a jigger of cognac. Fill the glass with shaved ice, shake until the ice is all dissolved, pour into a large goblet, fill up with ginger ale, stir, decorate and serve with straws.

182.   MAITRANK OR MAY-WINE.

GERMAN.

This drink is called May-wine because it is made from a shrub or plant (waldmeister), which is only to be procured in or about the month of May. At all other seasons of the year it does not possess the necessary fragrance, and is therefore never used. Place a quantity of waldmeister leaves in a pitcher and cover them with good white wine of any brand, allowing it to stand for twenty-four hours; sweeten to taste, strain, bottle, cork tightly and lay the bottles down in a cool place. This wine can be used for punches, cobblers, coolers or for any purpose for which white wine is recommended.

183.   MONTANA.

This name has been applied to bottled Pousse Café which is kept in second-class bars, or in establishments where incompetent or lazy bartenders are employed.

184.   NEAT.

The word "neat" is used in Great Britain to denote plain or straight in connection with the ordering of any liquor, as whiskey neat, meaning whiskey straight, etc., etc.

185.   ORANGEADE.

Take twelve drachms of concentrated infusion of orange peel, twelve drachms diluted sulphuric acid, five fluid ounces of syrup of orange peel and two gallons of water. Mix well and bottle. This is an excellent summer drink and is a sure cure for diarrhœa.

PICK ME UP. 186.

TO SOBER A DRUNK.

Place a jigger of Worcestershire sauce, a piece of ice and the juice of one lemon in a large glass and fill it with syphon soda or seltzer.

A strong cup of black coffee with a little salt in it is also a good Pick Me Up.

PONY. 187.

The word pony means small and is used in the ordering of a very small glass of any liquor. A pony glass is the smallest glass that is made; so, should you wish to serve a pony of any liquor, fill the smallest glass in the house with the desired brand and serve with ice water on the side. A neat way of serving a pony of any liquor is to place a small piece of ice in a small bar glass and pour the liquor from the pony glass over it, or place the small bar glass on the bar in front of the customer so he can have it as he desires.

PORT WINE NEGUS. 188.

Dissolve a teaspoonful of sugar in a little water in a small bar glass; add a piece of ice and a jigger of port wine and serve without decoration or spice.

POUSSE CAFÉ. 189.

FOUR-COLORED RAINBOW.

Pour the following ingredients carefully down the side of a small sherry glass and do not allow the different colors to mix: One-fourth glassful of raspberry syrup, crème de vanille or crème de cassis, one-fourth glassful of maraschino, one-fourth glassful of Chartreuse and one-fourth glassful of cognac. Serve ice water on the side.

POUSSE CAFÉ. 190.

NEW ORLEANS STYLE.

Make a Pousse Café from the preceding recipe and set the cognac afire before serving, allowing the fusil oil to consume; then immerse a piece of ice with a fruit or sugar tongs into the cognac to cool it and serve with ice water on the side.

191. ## POUSSE L'AMOUR.

Pour a little crême de vanille into a sherry glass, lay the yolk of an egg carefully on top of this, cover the yolk with maraschino and fill the glass with cognac.

192. ## QUEEN CHARLOTTE.

Place a piece of ice, a jigger of raspberry syrup and a dash of orgeat syrup in a large glass. Fill the glass with lemon soda or sweet soda and a little lemon juice, stir and serve.

193. ## RAFAEL NECTAR.

Into a large bar glass place a tablespoonful of sugar, two jiggers of sherry and a raw egg. Fill the glass with fine ice, shake thoroughly and serve in large goblet with fruits and straws.

194. ## RHINE WINE AND SELTZER.

Half fill a medium-size cut bar glass with cold Rhine wine and fill up the balance of the glass with syphon seltzer off the ice.

195. ## ROCK AND RYE.

Into a decanter of good rye whiskey place three or four sticks of rock candy and set it away for a few days before using. Serve the same as any plain liquor.

196. ## RUM AND GUM.

Pour about a teaspoonful of gum syrup into a small bar glass, place a toddy spoon in the glass, hand the customer a bottle of Jamaica rum so he can help himself, and serve ice water on the side.

SCAFFA. 197.

Fill a sherry glass with half maraschino and half cognac, add a few drops of Angostura bitters and serve ice water on the side. This drink is usually called a Brandy Scaffa.

SEIDLITZ POWDERS. 198.

These powders should be kept in every well-regulated bar. They are harmless when used properly, and are invaluable for settling a disordered stomach. Place twenty-five grains of carbonate of soda and three drachms of Rochelle salts in a blue paper and twenty grains of tartaric acid in a white paper and administer in the following manner. Dissolve the contents of the blue paper in a small bar glass of water and the powder contained in the white paper in a very large glass with a little water in the bottom. Now pour the contents of the small glass into the larger one and drink immediately while effervescing.

SETTLER. 199.

A name sometimes given to a mixture of equal parts of claret and plain soda.

SHANDY GAFF. 200.

This drink is a mixture of equal parts of ginger ale and ale, but lager beer can be substituted for ale if preferred.

SHERRY AND EGG. 201.

Dash a little sherry wine into a small bar glass; break an egg into another glass and if good throw in and place in front of customer with sherry bottle at his right so he can help himself. The idea of putting a little wine in the glass before placing the egg in was conceived for the purpose of preventing the egg from sticking to the glass while drinking.

202. SODA AND SYRUP.

Place a piece of ice and a dash of raspberry syrup in a medium-size glass; fill up with sweet soda and serve after stirring.

203. STARS AND STRIPES.

The English name for a pousse café. The idea of calling this popular French beverage by such a name originated once when a wag became intoxicated by an over-indulgence in these enticing mixtures, and declared that before partaking he had observed the most beautiful stripes, but afterward all he could see was stars. Hence the name "Stars and Stripes." (*See Recipe No. 189.*)

204. STICK.

A stick is a dash of whiskey added to any temperance drink.

205. STONE FENCE.

Into a small bar glass place a piece of ice and a jigger of whiskey, fill the glass with good cider and serve.

206. STONE WALL.

Another name for a Stone Fence.

207. SUNRISE.

Half fill a sherry glass with lime juice cordial and then carefully pour good cognac down the side of the glass until full. The cognac is set on fire before serving to destroy the fusil oil in the liquor. Always be careful not to allow the ingredients to run together, keeping the brandy on top.

THE BOY. 208.

An English term for champagne.

TOM COLLINS. 209.

Make the same as John Collins with Old Tom gin substituted for Holland gin. (*See Recipe No. 177.*)

TROTTER. 210.

A name sometimes given to a small milk punch. (*See Recipe No. 236.*)

UNFERMENTED WINE. 211.

FOR CHURCH USE.

Pick from the stems and weigh any quantity of grapes and cook with very little water, add one quarter as much sugar as you have used grapes and allow the mixture to simmer until the seeds, pulp and skins are all separated, strain through a muslin bag, bottle while warm and cork tightly.

VERMOUTH, GUM AND APOLLINARIS. 212.

A GREAT FRENCH BEVERAGE.

Into a long thin glass place a piece of ice, gum syrup to taste and a jigger of vermouth. Fill the glass with Apollinaris, stir and serve.

WATERMELON A LA MODE. 213.

THE LATEST FAD IN SWELLDOM.

Make a little less than a quart of good strong brandy punch, cut a hole in the end of a large ripe watermelon and save the piece which has been cut out; pour the punch slowly into the aperture until the melon has absorbed it all (it usually takes thirty minutes to acomplish this), replace the plug, ice the melon thoroughly, and when ready to serve cut into slices and serve on plates with knives, forks and napkins.

214. WHISKEY AND BITTERS.

Put a dash of Angostura bitters in a small bar glass and then throw it out, leaving only a little moisture in the glass. Hand a decanter or bottle of whiskey to the customer, allowing him to help himself, and serve ice water on the side.

215. WHISKEY AND GUM.

Place a dash of gum syrup in a small bar glass containing a spoon, hand the customer the whiskey and serve ice water on the side after stirring the drink.

216. WHISKEY AND SODA OR SELTZER.

Place a piece of ice in a long thin glass, hand the customer the desired liquor, and after he has helped himself fill the glass with syphon soda or seltzer.

217. WHISKEY AND SUGAR.

See Whiskey Toddy (*Recipe No. 304*).

218. WHITE SATIN.

An old British appellation for gin.

219. WHITE STRIPE.

FOR SORE THROAT.

Into a medium-size glass place about a tablespoonful of molasses, the juice of a large lemon and a piece of ice; fill the glass with white wine (any brand), stir until the molasses dissolves, and serve.

PUNCHES

APPLE PUNCH. 221.

Lay alternately in a large punch bowl slices of apples and lemons and strew each layer with powdered sugar. When the bowl is half full, pour a bottle of claret over the apples and lemons, cover with a clean cloth and allow it to stand five or six hours, after which strain through a muslin bag, ice and serve in cut glassware.

ARRACK PUNCH. 222.

Into a punch glass place a piece of ice and pour over it three-quarters jiggerful of Batavia arrack and one-quarter jiggerful of Jamaica rum. Then into a small mixing-glass place a large spoonful of sugar (as this punch needs much sweetening), the juice of one lime and a little Apollinaris. Stir until dissolved, pour into prepared punch glass, add a dash of California champagne, stir again, decorate and serve.

ARRACK PUNCH FOR A PARTY. 223.

ONE-HALF GALLON.

Cut six lemons into thin slices and remove the seeds. Place the slices into a vessel containing one quart of old Arrack and steep for five or six hours. Then carefully remove the slices without squeezing them. Then take about a pound of crushed sugar and boil in one quart of water, add the hot solution to the Arrack and let it cool. When you wish to serve this renowned beverage, place it in a punch bowl with a large piece of ice and decorate with fruits in season. A flavor of Jamaica rum is sometimes added.

224. BRANDY PUNCH.

Into a stem glass place a piece of ice, over which pour a jigger of cognac. Then take a small mixing-glass, into which place a large spoonful of sugar, the juice of one lemon, a dash of Curaçoa and a very little Apollinaris or plain water. Stir thouroughly, pour into the stem glass containing the ice and liquor, stir again, add a little fruit and serve. A dash of champagne is usually added.

225. BRANDY PUNCH.

FOR A PARTY OF TEN.

Into a large punch bowl place about one pound of sugar, three jiggerfuls of gum, one jiggerful of raspberry syrup, one jiggerful of Curaçoa, one jiggerful of maraschino and the juice of twenty limes. Pour in just enough Apollinaris to make the mixture dissolve, add a bottle and a half of good cognac and flavor with a wineglassful of Jamaica rum. Should the party be composed of any ladies, in place of a rum flavor a pint of champagne would be preferable. Place a large piece of ice in the bowl and decorate with fruits.

226. CHAMPAGNE PUNCH.

Into a punch bowl place five tablespoonfuls of sugar, the juice of ten lemons, a jigger of Curaçoa and a pony of maraschino. Dissolve in a small bottle of plain soda, add a quart of the desired brand of champagne and a large piece of ice. Decorate with fruits. Jamaica rum or good cognac can be used for a flavor. Either must be used, as champagne itself does not possess body enough to make a good punch.

227. CLARET PUNCH.

Place one tablespoonful of sugar and the juice of one lemon in a large mixing-glass. Fill the glass with fine ice and pour in as much claret as the glass will hold. Shake well, ornament with fruits and serve with straws.

CLARET PUNCH. 228.

FOR A PARTY.

Place six tablespoonfuls of sugar in a punch bowl and add the juice of six lemons and a small bottle of plain soda. Stir until dissolved, add a jigger of crême de vanille and one and one-half bottles of good claret. Stir, decorate, ice and serve in thin glassware. A pint of champagne poured over this punch just before serving is a great benefit to the flavor and adds life to it which it would not otherwise possess.

CREAM PUNCH. 229.

Into a large mixing-glass place a dessertspoonful of sugar, a jigger of cognac, a dash of St. Croix rum and some fine ice. Fill the glass with fresh cream, shake thoroughly, grate nutmeg over the top and serve with straws.

DRY PUNCH. 230.

Into a punch bowl place eight tablespoonfuls of sugar, the juice of ten limes, a jiggerful of Curaçoa and a quart of tea. Stir until the sugar is dissolved, add a bottle of cognac and a large piece of ice; decorate and serve in thin glassware. This punch may be bottled and kept for any length of time, and is said to improve with age. It is a very strong beverage, however; and a bottle of Apollinaris should be served with this punch (on the side), so that any member of the party who does not desire to partake of such an intoxicating mixture can dilute his drink with the queen of table waters.

FIRST INFT. REGT., N. G. C., PUNCH. 231.

Into a large punch bowl place one pound of sugar and the fresh juice of twenty limes. Add two jiggers of crême de vanille, one jigger of maraschino, one jigger of Curaçoa and a quart of Apollinaris. Stir until the sugar is thoroughly dissolved. Add two quarts of champagne and a half bottle of good cognac. Stir well, place a large lump of ice in the bowl and decorate with sliced pineapples, sliced seedless oranges, a few strawberries and a few sprigs of mint. Serve in thin glassware.

232.　　　　　　GOTHIC PUNCH.

Place twelve tablespoonfuls of bar sugar in a large punch bowl with the juice of a dozen limes. Dissolve in two bottles of Catawba wine and one bottle of good claret. Add a quart of champagne, a large lump of ice and some sliced pineapple. Serve in thin glassware.

233.　　　　HUB PUNCH, BOSTON STYLE.

Into a small cut bar glass place about two teaspoonfuls of gum syrup, the juice of one lemon, a piece of ice, a jigger of cognac and a dash of St. Croix rum. Stir, decorate and serve.

234.　　　　　　IMPERIAL PUNCH.

The proper way to brew this celebrated California beverage is to make it without the use of any water, and to use half champagne and half whiskey or brandy. Of course this makes a very rich and expensive drink as well as a very intoxicating one, but the following recipe is the correct thing, and has never been published before. Into a large punch goblet place two jiggers of whiskey or cognac (whichever the customer prefers) and a piece of ice about as large as an egg. Then place a tablespoonful of sugar in a medium-size mixing-glass with the juice of two limes. Add a little dash of Curaçoa and as much champagne as you have used liquor. Stir thoroughly and pour into the goblet of liquor and ice. Stir again and serve without decorations of any kind.

235.　　　　MAITRANK OR MAY-WINE PUNCH.

Into a large punch bowl place four tablespoonfuls of sugar, a jigger of maraschino, a jigger of Curaçoa, the juice of five lemons and a bottle of prepared May-wine (see Maitrank or May-wine). Stir until sugar is all dissolved, and place a large piece of ice in the bowl. When ready to serve add one-half syphon of seltzer and decorate with fruits. Serve in thin glassware.

236.　　　　　　MILK PUNCH.

Into a large mixing-glass place a dessertspoonful of sugar, a jigger of cognac and a dash of St. Croix rum, and fill the balance of the glass with good milk. Then place some cracked ice in a large shaker, shake well, pour into very large cut glass, grate nutmeg on top, and serve with straws.

MOUNTAINEER. 237.

A name sometimes given to a Milk Punch which has been frozen in the mixing-glass in the following manner: Make a milk punch according to the preceding recipe, with the ice in the glass. Shake well, stand the glass on the bar without removing the shaker for a few moments, and upon taking off the shaker a frosted foam will be seen on the top of the punch. Grate nutmeg over this and serve with straws.

NATIONAL GUARD PUNCH. 238.

See First Inft. Regt., N. G. C., Punch (*Recipe No. 231*).

ORCHARD PUNCH. 239.

Make the same as Orgeat Punch, substituting orchard syrup for orgeat. (*See Recipe No. 240.*)

ORGEAT PUNCH. 240.

Into a medium-size mixing-glass place a tablespoonful of orgeat syrup, the juice of two limes and a jigger of good cognac. Fill the glass with fine ice and stir well, pour into punch glass, dash with port wine, decorate with fruit and serve with straws.

PACIFIC-UNION CLUB PUNCH. 241.

FOR A PARTY OF TEN.

Into a large punch-bowl place ten tablespoonfuls of sugar and the fresh juice of ten good Sicily lemons. Add two jiggers of Curaçoa and two jiggers of crême de vanille, all dissolved in one quart of Apollinaris. Add two quarts of champagne and one bottle of Hennessey brandy. Place a large piece of ice in the bowl, decorate and serve in thin glassware.

242. ## REGENTS PUNCH.

FOR A LARGE PARTY.

Into a large punch-bowl place eight tablespoonfuls of sugar, the juice of ten lemons dissolved in a syphon of seltzer. Add three bottles of champagne, one of white wine (any brand), a wineglassful of Curaçoa, a bottle of cognac and dash with Jamaica rum. Stir well, decorate, ice and serve.

243. ## ROAD HOUSE PUNCH.

Heat a bottle of Burgundy in a hot-water urn. Add a little sugar and spice to taste, and serve in small silver covered mugs.

244. ## ROMAN PUNCH.

Into a medium-size bar glass place a spoonful of sugar, the juice of one lemon, a teaspoonful of raspberry syrup, a teaspoonful of Curaçoa and a jigger of cognac. Fill the glass with fine ice, stir well and strain into punch glass, dash with Jamaica rum and serve.

245. ## RUM PUNCH.

See St. Croix Punch (*Recipe No. 248*), and use the desired brand of rum in place of St. Croix.

246. ## SAUTERNE PUNCH.

Make the same as Claret Punch, substituting Sauterne for claret. A squirt of syphon seltzer improves this drink considerably. (*See Recipes Nos. 227–28.*)

247. ## SHERRY PUNCH.

Nearly fill a large mixing-glass with fine ice, add a spoonful of sugar, the juice of half a lime and a wineglassful of sherry. Shake well, strain into punch glass, decorate and serve.

ST. CROIX RUM PUNCH. 248.

Into a punch glass place a piece of ice and a jigger of St. Croix rum. Then place a spoonful of sugar and the juice of two limes in a medium-size mixing-glass, and dissolve in a little plain soda or seltzer (a dash of Curaçoa is usually added). Pour into the punch glass containing the rum and ice. Stir, decorate and serve.

TIP-TOP PUNCH. 249.

This term has been applied to many different decoctions by as many aspiring bartenders; but no beverage with this name ever became popular. Should any crank desire to have a tip-top punch brewed, by using any standard recipe for punches in this book his desires will be gratified, and he will declare his punch to be tip-top.

VANILLA CREAM PUNCH. 250.

Place a heaping teaspoonful of sugar in a large mixing-glass; add a jigger of cognac, a dash of St. Croix rum, and a pony of crème de vanille. Fill the glass with good cream, place some cracked ice in a large shaker, pour the contents of the mixing-glass into the shaker, shake well and serve in large cut glass with straws.

VANILLA PUNCH. 251.

Place a piece of ice and a jigger of cognac in a punch glass; then take a medium-size mixing-glass, and place in it a small spoonful of sugar, the juice of two limes and a pony of crème de vanille, dissolved in a little seltzer or plain water. Mix and pour over the cognac in the punch glass, decorate and serve.

VICTORIA PUNCH. 252.

This punch, like the Tip-top Punch, exists only in the imagination of a few over-ambitious bartenders; therefore, a recipe for making it is omitted, as only standard beverages are published herein.

253. <h2>WELLINGTON PUNCH.</h2>

This is a Brandy Punch flavored with a dash of strawberry syrup.

254. <h2>WHISKEY PUNCH.</h2>

Make the same as Brandy Punch, with whiskey substituted for cognac. (*See Recipes Nos. 224–25.*)

255. <h2>WHITE WINE PUNCH.</h2>

Make the same as Claret Punch, with the desired brand of white wine substituted for claret. (*See Recipes Nos. 227–28.*)

N. B.—A little effervescent water added to any white wine punch improves it greatly.

SANGAREES, COLD

ALE SANGAREE. 257.

Place a teaspoonful of sugar in a suitable glass and dissolve it in a jigger of water. Fill the glass with ale, grate nutmeg on top and serve.

BRANDY SANGAREE. 258.

Fill a large bar glass with fine ice, add a jigger of cognac and a spoonful of sugar, shake thoroughly, strain into a small cut glass, grate nutmeg on top and serve.

PORTER SANGAREE OR PORTEREE. 259.

The same as Ale Sangaree, with Dublin stout substituted for ale. (*See Recipe No. 257.*)

PORT WINE SANGAREE, COLD. 260.

Fill a medium-size mixing glass with fine ice, a spoonful of sugar and a wineglassful of port wine. Shake well, serve in thin glass with straws and grate nutmeg over the top.

WHISKEY SANGAREE. 261.

Make the same as Brandy Sangaree, with whiskey substituted for brandy. (*See Recipe No. 258.*)

WHITE WINE SANGAREE. 262.

Make the same as Port Wine Sangaree, with the desired brand of white wine substituted for port. (*See Recipe No. 260.*)

263.

SHAKES

264.   **BRANDY SHAKE.**

Into a small mixing-glass place a large spoonful of sugar and the juice of two limes. Fill the glass with fine ice and pour in a jigger of good cognac. Shake thoroughly, strain into small cut glass and serve.

265.   **GIN SHAKE.**

Make the same as Brandy Shake, with the desired brand of liquor substituted for cognac.

266.   **MILK SHAKE.**

Into a large mixing-glass place a spoonful of sugar and any kind of syrup which the customer prefers. Add a lump of ice and fill the glass with good milk. Shake well and serve.

267.   **RUM SHAKE.**

Make the same as Brandy Shake, with Jamaica rum substituted for brandy.

268.   **WHISKEY SHAKE.**

Make the same as Brandy Shake, with whiskey substituted for brandy.

 SHERBETS

ORANGE SHERBET. 270.

Dissolve one pound of sugar in two pints of water, and add the juice of two or three lemons and ten oranges. Strain through a muslin bag, and freeze in an ice-cream freezer.

PINEAPPLE SHERBET. 271.

Mix a pint of grated pineapple with a quart of water, the juice of three or four limes, and the whites of four eggs well beaten. Sweeten to taste, and freeze in ice-cream freezer.

TURKISH HAREM SHERBET. 272.

Place two or three slices of quince in a goblet of fine ice, and fill the glass with Vin de Rose. Decorate with pomegranate, and serve with straws. Quince essence may be substituted for sliced quince.

273.

SHRUBS

274. ### BRANDY SHRUB.

Into a vessel containing two quarts of cognac, place the juice of six good Sicily lemons and the peel of three. Cover for a few days, and add one quart of sherry and one and a half pounds of sugar. Strain through a jelly bag, and then bottle.

275. ### CHERRY SHRUB.

Place any quantity of cherries in an earthen pot, and place this pot in a large kettle of water. Cook over slow fire until all the juice is subtracted from the fruit; strain through muslin bag, sweeten to taste, and bottle with a glass of any kind of liquor in each bottle.

276. ### CURRANT SHRUB.

To one pint of currant juice add sweetening to taste. Boil gently for five or six minutes, skimming the while. When luke-warm add a wineglassful of liquor (whichever kind you prefer), and bottle.

277. ### RUM SHRUB.
ENGLISH STYLE.

To one quart of the juice of sour oranges add sugar to taste and one quart of Jamaica rum. This drink must be put away in a cool place for some weeks before using, as it improves with age.

278. ### SHRUBS OF ALL KINDS

May be properly prepared by substituting one liquor or one kind of fruit for another, and following the directions in the preceding recipes.

SLINGS, COLD

279.

BRANDY SLING. 280.

Dissolve a cube of sugar in a little water, and add a jigger of cognac and a piece of ice. Stir, grate nutmeg over the top, add a piece of lemon peel, and serve.

GIN SLING. 281.

Make the same as Brandy Sling, with Holland gin substituted for brandy.

RUM SLING. 282.

Make the same as Brandy Sling, with Jamaica rum substituted for brandy.

WHISKEY SLING. 283.

Make the same as Brandy Sling, with whiskey substituted for brandy.

284. # ✢ SMASHES ✤

285. ### BRANDY SMASH.

A small Mint Julep, with the rum flavor omitted. *(See Juleps, Recipes Nos. 114–19.)*

286. ### GIN SMASH.

A small Gin Julep. *(See Juleps.)*

287. ### RUM SMASH.

A small Rum Julep. *(See Juleps.)*

288. ### WHISKEY SMASH.

A small Whiskey Julep, with the rum flavor omitted. *(See Juleps.)*

⚜ SOURS ⚜

BRANDY SOUR. 290.

In the West it is customary to put a little lime juice in a small bar glass with a spoon; this is placed in front of the customer with the brandy bottle at his right hand, so he can help himself, and ice water is served on the side.

This is not a Brandy Sour, however, as the following directions for making that celebrated Eastern beverage will show :

Dissolve in a medium-size mixing-glass one dessertspoonful of sugar, the juice of one good lemon, a squirt of syphon seltzer, and a jigger of the desired liquor. Nearly fill the glass with cracked ice, stir and strain into punch glass, decorate and serve.

GIN SOUR. 291.

Make the same as Brandy Sour with Holland gin substituted for brandy.

RUM SOUR. 292.

Make the same as Brandy Sour, with Jamaica rum substituted for brandy.

ST. CROIX SOUR. 293.

Make the same as Brandy Sour, with St. Croix rum substituted for brandy.

WHISKEY SOUR. 294.

Make the same as Brandy Sour, with whiskey substituted for brandy.

295.  **STRAIGHTS**

296. BRANDY STRAIGHT.

Set a small bar glass on the bar in front of a customer with the brandy bottle at his right, allowing him to help himself.   Serve ice water on the side.

297. GIN STRAIGHT.

The same as Brandy Straight with Holland gin substituted for brandy.

298. RUM STRAIGHT.

The same as Brandy Straight, with Jamaica rum substituted for brandy.

299. WHISKEY STRAIGHT.

The same as Brandy Straight, with the desired brand of liquor substituted for brandy.

TODDIES, COLD

300.

BRANDY TODDY. 301.

Place half a teaspoonful of sugar in a small bar glass, and dissolve it in about two teaspoonfuls of water; leave a small spoon in the glass and hand the customer a bottle of cognac, allowing him to help himself. Serve ice water on the side.

GIN TODDY. 302.

Make the same as Brandy Toddy, with Holland Gin substituted for cognac.

SOFT TODDY. 303.

(CALIFORNIA STYLE.)

Cut the peel off half a lemon (the skin of a lime should never be used), and place it in a small mixing-glass with a dessertspoonful of sugar and a little water; mash the lemon peel with a muddler until all the extract of the skin has been absorbed by the sugar and water. Then place a small piece of ice in a small cut bar glass, and pour a jigger of whiskey over it; then add the lemon-peel, sugar and water, grate nutmeg over the top and serve.

WHISKEY TODDY. 304.

Make the same as Brandy Toddy, with whiskey substituted for brandy.

Valuable Secrets for Liquor Dealers.

306. ADULTERATION AND AGEING OF WHISKEY.

The following recipe is for a simple process, by which new whiskey may be made to appear and taste like old. To each barrel of whiskey add three-quarters of a gallon of prune juice (a concoction made of steamed prunes, blood, spirits and sugar); it will then have the color and flavor of three-year-old whiskey; more may be added in proper proportion to any age desired up to ten years.

307. ALCOHOLIZING OF WINES.

Alcohol added to weak or vapid wines will increase their strength and assist in their preservation. It can be added to port in the ratio of one part alcohol to two parts port; to sherry, one part alcohol to seven parts sherry; and to other wines in proportion to the strength of their flavor.

308. BATAVIA ARRACK.

To twelve gallons of pale rum add two ounces of flowers of Benzoin, half an ounce of balsam of Tolu, and one ounce of sliced pineapples. Digest with an occasional agitation for one month, at the end of which time add half a pint of milk. Agitate for ten minutes, and rack off in a week.

BEAD FOR LIQUOR. 309.

The best bead is orange-flower water (oil of neroil), one drop to each gallon.

Another method : For every ten gallons of spirit add forty drops of sulphuric acid and sixty drops of olive oil previously mixed in a glass vessel. This must be used immediately.

Another good recipe : Take one ounce of the purest oil of sweet almonds, and one ounce of sulphuric acid; put them in a stone mortar and add, by degrees, two ounces of white lump sugar, rubbing it well with the pestle until it becomes a paste; then add small quantities of spirits of wine until it becomes a liquid. This quantity is sufficient for one hundred gallons. The first recipe is the best, however.

BLACKBERRY BRANDY. 310.

Macerate a pint of fine ripe blackberries (mashed) in one gallon of cognac for one week. Sweeten to taste, filter and bottle. Any kind of berries can be treated in the same manner.

BOTTLED SODA WATER WITHOUT A MACHINE. 311.

Sweeten a gallon of water to taste, and put it into soda bottles. Into each bottle drop half a drachm of bi-carbonate of soda and half a drachm of citric acid (crystallized). Cork immediately, and tie the corks securely.

BOTTLING OF WINES. 312.

To bottle wine successfully, great pains must be taken to have the bottles and corks scrupulously clean, and to carefully refrain from jarring the barrel, or agitating its contents, so the sediment will not be disturbed. After bottling, lay the bottles down in a cool place. (*See Corking, Recipe No. 328.*)

BOURBON WHISKEY. 313.

To one hundred gallons of proof spirit, add four ounces of pear oil, two ounces of pelargonif ether, thirteen drachms of oil of wintergreen (dissolved in the ether), and one gallon of wine vinegar. Color with burnt sugar.

314.   BRANDY.

To forty gallons of pure or neutral spirits, add one pound of crude tartar dissolved in one gallon of hot water; acetic ether one-quarter pint; bruised raisins, six pounds; tincture of kino, two ounces, and sugar, three pounds. Color with burnt sugar. Let it stand two weeks, and then draw it off.

315.   BRANDY BITTERS.

Bruised gentian, eight ounces; orange peel, five ounces; cardamoms, three ounces; cassia, one ounce; cochineal, one-quarter ounce; and spirit, one gallon. Digest for one week, then decant the clear, and pour five pints of water on the dregs. Digest for one week longer, decant, and mix the two tinctures together.

316.   BRITISH CHAMPAGNE.

Loaf sugar, fifty-six pounds; brown sugar (pale), forty-eight pounds; warm water, forty-five gallons; white tartar, four ounces. Mix, and at a proper temperature add one quart of yeast, five gallons of sweet cider, six or seven bruised bitter almonds, one gallon of pale spirit, and half an ounce of orris powder.

317.   BRITISH COGNAC BRANDY.

One hundred gallons of clean spirit (seventeen up), ten gallons of highly flavored cognac, one and a half ounces of oil of cassia, half an ounce of oil of bitter almonds, ten ounces of powdered catechu, sixteen ounces of cream of tartar (dissolved), three pounds of Beaufoy's concentrated acetic acid, and about a quart of sugar coloring. Put the whole into a fresh-emptied brandy-piece, and let them remain about a week with a little agitation occasionally, then let them stand to settle.

CASKINESS. 318.

Caskiness is caused by wine being put into a dirty cask or into one that has been unused for a long time. It can be removed by vigorously agitating the wine for some time with a little sweet or almond oil. The cause of the bad taste is the presence of an essential oil, which the fixed oil combines with and carries to the surface, from whence it can be skimmed off or the wine be drawn off beneath it. A little coarsely powdered, freshly burnt charcoal, or some slices of bread toasted black, or bruised mustard seed, sometimes effect the removal of the objectionable taste.

CEMENT FOR BOTTLES. 319.

Melt together one-quarter pound of resin and a couple of ounces of beeswax; when it froths, stir it with a tallow candle, and, as soon as it melts, dip the mouths of the corked bottles into it.

CHEAP BEER. 320.

Fill a boiler with the green shells of peas, pour on water till it rises half an inch above the shells, and simmer for three hours. Strain off the liquor, and add a strong decoction of the wood sage or the hop, so as to render it pleasantly bitter, then ferment in the usual manner. The wood sage is the best substitute for hops, and being free from any anodyne property is entitled to a preference. By boiling a fresh quantity of shells in the decoction before it becomes cold, it may be so thoroughly impregnated with saccharine matter as to afford a liquor, when fermented, as strong as ale.

CIDER CHAMPAGNE. 321.

Good cider, twenty gallons; spirit, one gallon; honey or sugar, six pounds. Mix and let them rest for a fortnight; then fine with skimmed milk, one quart. Bottle well and tie corks securely, as after being bottled for some time it becomes very lively.

Another good recipe: Good pale vinous cider, 1 hogshead; proof spirit (pale), 3 gallons; honey or sugar, 14 lbs. Mix, and let them remain together in a temperate situation for one month; then add orange-flower water, 1 quart; and fine it down with skimmed milk, ½ a gallon. This will be very pale; and a similar article, when bottled in champagne bottles, silvered and labeled, has been often sold to the ignorant for Champagne It opens very brisk, if managed properly.

322.   CIDER—TO KEEP SWEET.

1st. By putting into the barrel before the cider has begun to work about a half pint of whole fresh mustard seed tied up in a coarse muslin bag.   2d. By burning a little sulphur or sulphur match in the barrel previous to putting in the cider.   3d. By the use of ¾ of an ounce of the bi-sulphite of lime to the barrel. This article is the preserving powder sold at rather a high price by various firms.

323   CIDER WITHOUT APPLES.

To each gallon of cold water put one pound common sugar, one-half ounce tartaric acid, one tablespoonful of yeast.   Shake well, make in the evening and it will be fit for use next day.   I make in a keg a few gallons at a time, leaving a few quarts to make into next time, not using yeast again until the keg needs rinsing.   If it gets a little sour make a little more into it, or put as much water with it as there is cider, and put it with the vinegar.   If it is desired to bottle this cider by manufacturers of small drinks, you will proceed as follows :   Put in a barrel five gallons hot water, thirty pounds brown sugar, three-quarters pound tartaric acid, twenty-five gallons cold water, three pints of hop or brewers' yeast worked into paste with three-quarters pound flour ; and one pint water will be required in making this paste. Put all together in a barrel, which it will fill, and let it work twenty-four hours,—the yeast running out at the bung all the time by putting in a little occasionally to keep it full.   Then bottle, putting in two or three broken raisins in each bottle, and it will nearly equal champagne.

324.   CLARIFYING OF WINES.

To each gallon of wine one ounce of pure strained honey should be used. Take as many ounces of honey as there are gallons of wine to be clarified ; heat to nearly a boiling point with some of the wine, and then allow the blend to cool before adding it to the wine.   Agitate the barrel well, and then let it stand for at least one month, after which the wine should be drawn off very carefully.

325.   COGNAC.

To every ten gallons of pure spirits add two quarts of New England rum or one quart of Jamaica rum, and from thirty to forty drops of oil cognac put in half a pint of alcohol. Color with sugar coloring.

COLORING. 326.

Place two pounds of crushed or lump sugar into a kettle that will hold four or five quarts with half a tumbler of water. Boil until it is black, then take it off the fire, and cool it by pouring in cold water, stirring the while.

CORDIAL GIN. 327.

Oil of bitter almonds, vitriol, turpentine and juniper, one-half drachm each; kill the oils in spirits of wine; fifteen gallons of clean, rectified proof spirits, to which add one drachm of coriander seeds, one drachm of pulverized orris root, one-half pint of elder-flower water, with ten pounds of sugar, and five gallons of water or liquor.

CORKING. 328.

Before using corks be sure to have them clean. To drive a large cork into a small bottle neck, or a silver-topped patent cork, soak them thoroughly in boiling water, when they will become soft and pliable. A wooden cork-driver and mallet are used for driving them into bottles. When corking wine, always dip each cork separately in cognac just before driving it into the bottle

CRÊME DE MÊNTHE. 329.

Macerate for a couple of days, in one gallon of alcohol, four pounds of peppermint leaves and the skins of a dozen lemons. Strain, add three gallons of water, and sweeten to taste.

CURE FOR DRUNKENNESS. 330.

Spirit of nutmeg, one drachm; peppermint water, eleven drachms; sulphate of iron, five grains; magnesia, ten grains. Twice a day.

This preparation acts as a tonic and stimulant, and so partially supplies the place of the accustomed liquor, and prevents that absolute physical and moral prostration that follows a sudden breaking off from the use of stimulating drinks.

Captain John Vine Hall, Commander of the famous steamship *Great Eastern*, was cured of habitual intoxication by using this recipe, and published the fact for the benefit of humanity in the English press some years ago.

331.   DAMIANA BITTERS.

Macerate for fourteen days any quantity of Damiana roots in just enough alcohol to cover them, reduce to any desired strength with water, flavor with cardamom seed, clarify and bottle.

332.   DECANTING.

When decanting any wine or liquor, great care should be observed in preventing any sediment or crust from entering the decanter. A good plan is to filter through filtering paper or fine cambric, and not to drain too closely.

333. DUTIES ON FOREIGN WINES, LIQUORS, ETC.

(NEW TARIFF.)

1891.

SCHEDULE H.

SPIRITS.

	Old Rate.	New Rate.
Anhydrous alcohol, per gallon	$1 00	$2 50
Brandy and spirits, distilled, per gallon	2 00	2 50

Each and every gauge or wine gallon of measurement shall be counted as at least one proof gallon, and the standard for determining the proof of brandy and other spirits or liquors of any kind imported shall be the same as that which is defined in the laws relating to internal revenue; but any brandy or other spirituous liquors, imported in casks of less capacity than fourteen gallons, shall be forfeited to the United States; provided, that it shall be lawful for the Secretary of the Treasury, in his discretion, to authorize the ascertainment of the proof of wines, cordials or other liquors, by distillation or otherwise, in case where it is impracticable to ascertain such proof by the means prescribed by existing law or regulations.

On all compounds or preparations of which distilled spirits are a component part of chief value, not specially provided for in this Act, there shall be levied a duty not less than that imposed upon distilled spirits.

Cordials, liquors, arrack, absinthe, kirschwasser, ratafia, and other spirituous beverages or bitters of all kinds containing spirits, per gallon *Old Rate.* $2 00 *New Rate.* $2 50

No lower rate or amount of duty shall be levied, collected and paid on brandy, spirits and other spirituous beverages than that fixed by law for the description of first proof; but it shall be increased in proportion for any greater strength than the strength of the first proof; and all imitations of brandy or spirits or wines imported by any names whatever shall be subject to the highest rate of duty provided for the genuine articles respectively intended to be represented, and in no case less than **$1.50** per gallon.

Bay rum or bay water of first proof and in proportion for any greater strength than first proof, per gallon.........

	Old Rate.	New Rate.
Bay rum or bay water... per gallon	$1 00	$1 50

WINES.

	Old Rate.	New Rate.
Champagnes and sparkling wines in bottles from 1 pint to 1 quart, per dozen	$7 00	$8 00
One-half pint to 1 pint, per dozen	3 50	4 00
One-half pint or less, per dozen	1 75	2 00
More than 1 quart, in addition, on quantity in excess, per gallon	2 25	2 50
Still wines in casks, per gallon	50	50
Ginger wine in casks, per gallon	20 p c	50
Still wines in bottles, per case of 1 dozen quarts or 2 dozen half quarts	1 60	1 60
Any excess found on such excess, per pint	05	05

Provided that any wines, ginger cordial or vermouth imported containing more than twenty-four per cent of alcohol shall be forfeited to the United States; and provided further, that there shall be no constructive or other allowance for breakage, leakage or damage on wines, liquors, cordials or distilled spirits. Wines, cordials, brandy and other spirituous liquors imported in bottles or jugs shall be packed in packages containing not less than one dozen bottles or jugs in each package; and all such bottles or jugs shall pay an additional duty of three cents for each bottle or jug containing more than one pint, and two cents each on bottles or jugs containing one pint or less.

	Old Rate.	New Rate.
Ale, porter and beer, in bottles or jugs, per gallon	35c	40c
Otherwise than bottles and jugs, per gallon	20c	35c
Malt extract, fluid, in casks, per gallon	20 p c	20c
In bottles or jugs, per gallon	20 p c	40c
Solid or condensed	20 p c	40 p c
Cherry juice, prune wine, fruit juice, not containing more than 18 per cent of alcohol, per gallon	20 p c	60c
More than 18 per cent of alcohol, per gallon	20 p c	{ $2 50 / 25 p c
Ginger ale, in plain ¾ pint bottles, per dozen	20 p c	13c
Lemonade and other artificial waters, in same, per dozen	30 p c	13c
Ginger ale, in ¾ to 1½ pint bottles, per dozen	20 p c	26c
Lemonade, etc., in same, per dozen	30 p c	26c
Ginger ale, otherwise than in plain bottles or more than 1½ pint bottles, per gallon	20 p c	50c
Lemonade, if same, per gallon	30 p c	50c
Mineral waters, in pint bottles, per dozen	20 p c	16c
1 pint to 1 quart, per dozen	20 p c	25c
Over 1 quart, per gallon	20 p c	20c

(In addition thereto duty shall be collected on all above bottles at rates chargeable if imported empty.)

334.   ENGLISH GIN.

To one hundred gallons of plain malt spirit add one pint of spirits of turpentine and seven pounds of Bay salt; mix and distil.   The difference in the flavor of gin is produced by varying the proportion of turpentine, and occasionally adding a small quantity of juniper berries.

335.   FINING OF WINES.

If the racked wine is not clear it is fined by the addition of isinglass previously softened by soaking in a small quantity of wine.   After the isinglass has been added, agitate the barrel and contents well, and then bung close (being careful to have it filled to the bung).   Do not draw off for at least four weeks.   Should a second fining be necessary, a little sweet milk may be added.

336.   FRENCH BRANDY.

To every gallon of pure spirits add one quart of the kind of brandy which you wish to imitate, two ounces of loaf sugar, half an ounce of sweet spirits of niter, and a few drops of tincture of catechu or oak bark to roughen the taste if desired; color with burnt sugar.

337.   FUSIL OIL.
HOW TO DESTROY ITS PRESENCE IN LIQUORS.

Add one-half pint of spirits of wine, one pound of unslacked lime and half a pound of powdered alum to forty gallons of whiskey.   Stir thoroughly and then allow it to settle for a couple of days.   This treatment precipitates the verdigris to the bottom; therefore the sediment should be handled with great caution.

338.   GIN.

To one hundred gallons of clear, rectified spirits add, after you have killed the oil well, one and a half ounces of the oil of English juniper, half an ounce of angelica essence, half an ounce of oil of bitter almonds, one-half ounce of the oil of coriander, and one-half ounce of the oil of caraway. Rummage this up and you have what rectifiers call strong gin.   To make this up as it is called by the trade, add forty-five pounds of loaf sugar (dissolved).   Rummage the whole well up together with four ounces of roche alum.   Two ounces of salts of tartar may be added for finings.

GINGER BEER. 339.

Ten pounds of sugar, nine ounces of lemon juice, half a pound of honey, eleven ounces of bruised ginger root, nine gallons of water and three pints of yeast. Boil the ginger for a half hour in a gallon of water; then add the rest of the water and the other ingredients, and strain it when cold. Add the white of an egg beaten and half an ounce of essence of lemon. Let it stand four days, then bottle and it will keep many months.

GINGER WINE. 340.

Place one ounce of best bruised ginger root into a vessel containing one quart of ninety-five per cent alcohol, five grains of capsicum and one drachm of tartaric acid. Let it stand several days and then filter it. Now add one gallon of water in which one pound of crushed sugar has been boiled; mix when cold. To make the color, boil half an ounce of cochineal, three-quarter ounce of cream of tartar, half an ounce of saleratus and half an ounce of alum in a pint of water until you get a bright red color.

GOLDWASSER. 341.

Dissolve four drops of oil of cinnamon, twelve drops of anise seed, two drachms of mace, six drops of oil of citron and four drops of oil of roses in one quart of pure spirit. After standing eight or ten days, strain with pressure through a cloth bag, and then filter. Now add one quart of simple syrup and some bits of gold leaf. This is a valuable recipe.

HOLLAND GIN. 342.

Add two ounces of spirits of niter, four pounds of loaf sugar, one ounce oil of juniper and one-eighth ounce oil of caraway to forty gallons of neutral spirits. The juniper and caraway to be first cut in one quart of alcohol and allowed to stand for twenty-four hours before adding to the other iugredients.

343. IRISH WHISKEY.

To forty gallons of proof spirits add sixty drops of creosote dissolved in one quart of alcohol, two ounces of acetic acid and one pound of loaf sugar. Let it stand two or three days before using.

344. JAMAICA RUM.

To forty-five gallons of New England rum add five gallons of Jamaica rum, two ounces of butyric ether, half an ounce of oil of caraway cut with alcohol (ninety-five per cent) and color with sugar coloring.

Another good recipe: To thirty-six gallons of pure spirits add one gallon of Jamaica rum, three ounces of butyric ether, three ounces of acetic ether and half a gallon of sugar syrup. Mix the ethers and acid with the Jamaica rum and stir it well with the spirit. Color with burnt sugar.

345. KOUMISS OR MILK CHAMPAGNE.

The Bashkirs are renowned for their skill in making Koumiss or fermented mares' milk, which is now extensively used by consumptives and persons afflicted by wasting and dyspeptic diseases. So easy is it of digestion, that invalids drink ten and fifteen champagne bottles full every day; while a Bashkir is able to overcome a couple of gallons at a sitting, and in an hour or two to be ready for more.

To insure good Koumiss it is essential that the mares be of the steppe breed and fed on steppe pasture. They are milked from four to six times a day, the foal being kept apart from the mother and allowed to suck only in the night-time. The mare will not give her milk, however, unless, at the time of milking, her foal is brought to her side, when such is the joy of the reunion, that after sundry acts of loving, smelling and kissing, the maternal feeling shows itself by her sometimes giving milk from both nipples at once. Milking is done by Bashkir women who, taking a position close to the hind legs of the mare, rest on one knee, and on the other support a pail directly under the udder, pulling at each nipple in turn, and receiving from three to four pints at a milking.

To make Koumiss the milk is beaten up in a churn (but not sufficiently to make butter), and by fermentation is converted after twenty-four hours into weak Koumiss, from which condition it passes after twelve hours more to a medium degree of strength; whilst strong Koumiss is produced by assiduous agitation of the milk for two or three days, when it is said to be slightly intoxicating.

A good imitation of this very high-priced luxury can be produced as follows : Into a champagne or syphon soda bottle place a cube of fresh compressed yeast (if this cannot be procured two ounces of fresh yeast will answer the purpose) and three tablespoonfuls of bar sugar. (This may appear to be too much sugar, but considerble sweetening is necessary to overcome the taste of the yeast). Fill the bottle with good, sweet milk, and if a champagne bottle is used, tie the cork securely. Lay the bottle down in a warm place for a day, then lay it in a cool place for four days before using. Should a syphon bottle be used, sufficient gas will generate in the bottle to cause the Koumiss to flow like soda.

MADEIRA WINE. 346.

To forty gallons of prepared cider add one-quarter pound of tartaric acid, four gallons of spirits and three pounds of loaf sugar. Let it stand for ten days, draw it off carefully, fine it down and then rack it again into another cask.

MEAD. 347.

The following is a good recipe for mead : On twenty pounds of honey pour five gallons of boiling water; boil, and remove the scum as it rises; add one ounce of best hops, and boil for ten minutes; then put the liquor into a tub to cool; when all but cold add a little yeast spread upon a slice of toasted bread; let it stand in a warm room. When fermentation is set up, put the mixture into a cask, and fill up from time to time as the yeast runs out of the bunghole; when the fermentation is finished, bung it down, leaving a peg-hole which can afterwards be closed, and in less than a year it will be fit to bottle.

MONONGAHELA WHISKEY. 348.

To forty gallons of proof spirits add two ounces spirits of niter, four pounds of dried peaches, four pounds N. O. sugar, one quart of rye (burnt and ground like coffee), one-quarter pound allspice, half a pound of cinnamon and half a pound of cloves. Put in the ingredients, and after standing five days draw it off and strain.

349. **PALE BRANDY.**

Pure spirits, one gallon; the kind of pale brandy you wish to imitate, one quart; loaf sugar, two ounces; sweet spirits of niter, one-half ounce; tincture of kino, two drachms; and two drops of tincture of catechu to roughen the taste if desired; color to suit and filter.

350. **PINEAPPLE RUM.**

To fifty gallons of rum made by the fruit method add twenty-five pine-apples sliced, and eight pounds of white sugar. Let it stand two weeks before drawing off.

351. **PORT WINE.**

Worked cider, forty-two gallons; good port wine, twelve gallons; good brandy, three gallons; pure spirits, six gallons; mix. Elderberries and sloes and the fruit of the black hawes make a fine purple color for wines, or use burnt sugar.

352. **ROOT BEER.**

For each gallon of water to be used, take hops, burdock, yellow dock, sarsaparilla, dandelion and spikenard roots, bruised, of each one-half ounce; boil about twenty minutes and strain while hot; add eight or ten drops of oils of spruce and sassafras mixed in equal proportions; when cool enough not to scald your hand, put in two or three tablespoons of yeast; molasses, three-eighths of a pint, or white sugar, one-half pound, gives it about the right sweetness.

353. **RYE WHISKEY.**

Bake, scorch and roast half a peck of dried peaches in an oven, but don't burn them. Bruise and put them in a woolen bag, and pour good whiskey over them several times. Add afterwards twelve drops of ammonia to each barrel, and, with ageing essence, you will have whiskey equal to old rye.

SANTA CRUZ OR ST. CROIX RUM. 354.

Add five gallons of Santa Cruz rum, five pounds of crushed sugar dissolved in four quarts of water, three ounces of butyric acid, and two ounces of acetic ether to fifty gallons of pure proof spirit. Color if necessary.

SCHIEDAM SCHNAPPS. 355.

(A FINE IMITATION.)

To twenty-five gallons of good Holland gin (five over proof), add fifteen pints of strained honey, two gallons of clear water, five pints of white sugar syrup, five pints spirit of nutmeg, five pints orange-flower water, seven quarts of pure water, one ounce of acetic ether, and eight drops oil of wintergreen dissolved with the ether. Mix well, and if fining be necessary use alum and salt of tartar.

SCOTCH WHISKEY. 356.

Into a large cask pour one-quarter of a barrel of Scotch whiskey, one-half of a barrel of pure spirit (ten over proof), three drops of creosote mixed with one ounce of acetic acid and one ounce of pelargonic ether. Irish whiskey may be made by substituting Irish for Scotch.

NOTE.—A few drops of creosote dissolved in one-quarter ounce of acetic ether and added to three gallons of Holland gin makes a fine imitation of Scotch whiskey.

SHERRY. 357.

To forty gallons of prepared cider, add two gallons of spirits, three pounds of raisins, six gallons of good sherry, and half an ounce of bitter almonds oil (dissolved in alcohol). Let it stand ten days, and draw it off carefully; fine it down, and again rack it into another cask.

358. SPRUCE BEER.

Take of the essence of spruce half a pint; bruised pimento and ginger, of each four ounces; water, three gallons. Boil five or ten minutes, then strain and add eleven gallons of warm water, a pint of yeast, and six pints of molasses. Allow the mixture to ferment for twenty-four hours.

359. STOMACH BITTERS.

(EQUAL TO HOSTETTER'S.)

European Gentian root, 1½ ounces; orange peel, 2½ ounces; cinnamon, ¼ ounce; anise seed, ½ ounce; coriander seed, ½ ounce; cardamom seed, ⅛ ounce; unground Peruvian bark, ½ ounce; gum kino, ¼ ounce; bruise all these articles, and put them into the best alcohol, 1 pint; let it stand a week, and pour off the clear tincture; then boil the dregs a few minutes in 1 quart of water, strain, and press out all the strength; now dissolve loaf sugar, 1 pound, in the hot liquid, adding 3 quarts cold water, and mix with spirit tincture first poured off, filter and bottle.

360. STRONG BEER.

(A VALUABLE ENGLISH RECIPE.)

Malt, 1 peck; coarse brown sugar, 6 pounds; hops, 4 ounces; good yeast, 1 teacup; if you have not malt, take a little over 1 peck of barley (twice the amount of oats will do, but are not as good), and put it into an oven after the bread is drawn, or into a stove oven, and steam the moisture from them. Grind coarsely. Now pour upon the ground malt 3½ gallons of water at 170 or 172 degrees of heat. The tub in which you scald the malt should have a false bottom, two or three inches from the real bottom; the false bottom should be bored full of gimlet holes, so as to act as a strainer to keep back the malt meal. When the water is poured on, stir them well, and let it stand 3 hours, and draw off by a faucet; put in 7 gallons more of water at 180 to 182 degrees; stir it well, and let it stand 2 hours, and draw it off; then put on a gallon or two of cold water, stir it well and draw it off. You should have about five or six gallons. Put the six pounds of coarse brown sugar in an equal amount of water; mix with the wort, and boil 1½ to 2 hours with the hops. You should have eight gallons when boiled; when cooled to 80 degrees put in the yeast, and let it work 18 to 20 hours, covered with a sack; use sound iron-hooped kegs or porter bottles, bung or cork tight, and in two weeks it will be good sound beer, and will keep a long time; and for persons of a weak habit of body, and especially females, one glass of this with their meals is far better than tea or coffee, or all the ardent spirits in the universe. If more malt is used, not exceeding ½ a bushel, the beer, of course, would have more spirit; but this strength is sufficient for the use of females or invalids.

SYRUPS.   361.

Syrups are made by using loaf or crushed sugar, 8 pounds; pure water, 1 gallon; gum arabic, 2 ounces; mix in a brass or copper kettle; boil until the gum is dissolved, then skim and strain through white flannel, after which add tartaric acid, $5\frac{1}{2}$ ounces dissolved in hot water; to flavor, use extract of lemon, orange, rose, pine-apple, peach, sarsaparilla, strawberry, etc., $\frac{1}{2}$ ounce to each bottle, or to your taste.

Taxes on Liquors, Etc.

[*Internal Revenue.—Form No. II.—Revised Dec., 1886.*]

THE FOLLOWING ARE

THE SPECIAL TAXES

NOW IMPOSED BY LAW, TO WIT:

Rectifiers of less than 500 barrels	$100 00
Rectifiers of 500 barrels or more	200 00
Dealers, retail liquor	25 00
Dealers, wholesale liquor	100 00
Dealers in malt liquors, wholesale	50 00
Dealers in malt liquors, retail	20 00
Dealers in leaf tobacco	12 00
Dealers in leaf tobacco received from producers in "the hand," less than 25,000 pounds per annum	5 00
Retail dealers in leaf tobacco	250 00
and on monthly sales over rate of $500 per annum, thirty cents for every dollar in excess of such rate.	
Dealers in manufactured tobacco	2 40
Retail dealers in oleomargarine	48 00
Wholesale dealers in oleomargarine	480 00
Manufacturers of oleomargarine	600 00
Manufacturers of oleomargarine commencing business subsequent to the thirtieth day of June in any year	500 00
Manufacturers of stills	50 00
and for each still manufactured	20 00
and for each worm manufactured	20 00
Manufacturers of tobacco	6 00
Manufacturers of cigars	6 00
Peddlers of tobacco, first class (more than two horses or other animals)	30 00
Peddlers of tobacco, second class (two horses or other animals)	15 00
Peddlers of tobacco, third class (one horse or other animal)	7 20
Peddlers of tobacco, fourth class (on foot or public conveyance)	3 60
Brewers of less than 500 barrels	50 00
Brewers of 500 barrels or more	100 00

INSTRUCTIONS TO SPECIAL-TAX PAYERS.

I.

The special-tax year commences on the first day of May and ends on the 30th day of April succeeding.

II.

Applicants for a special tax for a fractional part of a year must calculate from the first day of the month in which they commence business to the end of the special-tax year, except manufacturers of oleomargarine who commence business on or after the first day of July, who will be liable from July 1st.

III.

Retail dealers in malt liquors cannot retail spirituous liquors or wines without paying special tax as retail liquor dealers.

IV.

Retail liquor dealers cannot, as such, sell five gallons to one person at any one time. Any person desiring to sell in quantities of five or more gallons must make this return and pay the special tax as a wholesale liquor dealer. The word "gallon" here used means "wine-gallon."

V.

No dealer in wines, spirits, or malt liquors can lawfully sell manufactured or leaf tobacco, snuff or cigars without previously paying the special tax as a dealer in manufactured or leaf tobacco, as the case may be.

VI.

Rectifiers or brewers who have paid special tax as "rectifiers or brewers of less than 500 barrels," and who, during the same special-tax year, desire to increase their product, should make application hereon for a new stamp of the denomination of $200 in the case of a rectifier, or $100 in the case of a brewer. On obtaining this new stamp the rectifier or brewer may apply to the Commissioner of Internal Revenue, under section 3426, Revised Statutes, for the repayment to him of the value of the stamp first issued, less five per cent deduction therefrom.

VII.

Dealers in leaf tobacco received from producers, etc., in the hand, as provided in act of June 16, 1880, the amount of whose sales, consignments, or offers for sale exceed 25,000 lbs. in the aggregate in any special-tax year, must pay $12 tax as "Dealer in leaf tobacco."

VIII.

Manufacturers and wholesale dealers may sell oleomargarine only in original stamped packages of not less than ten pounds. A retail dealer must sell only from original stamped packages in quantities of not more than ten pounds, packed in new wooden or paper packages marked with his name and address, and the word " *Oleomargarine* " in large letters written or printed thereon. (See section 6, act of Aug. 2, 1886.)

IX.

Special-tax stamps are not transferrable from one dealer to another. When a new member is added to a firm paying special tax, a new stamp will be required.

X.

Special-tax stamps will be transmitted by mail only on receipt, from the person or firm ordering the same, of specific directions so to do. If it is desired that they be transmitted by *registered* mail, *ten cents* additional should accompany the application.

☞ POSTAGE STAMPS will not be received in payment of special taxes.

Every person or firm liable to special tax must, before commencing business, file, and thereafter, while thus liable, not later than the 30th day of April of each year, again file with the Collector or Deputy Collector a sworn return (in legal form), and pay to such officer the amount of the tax, when he will be furnished with a *Special-tax stamp*, which must at all times be conspicuously displayed in his, or their, place of business. For failure to make the return as above stated, the Commissioner of Internal Revenue is required by law (section 3176, Revised Statutes) to assess a penalty of fifty per centum of the entire amount of the special tax. The failure to procure a special-tax stamp also renders the delinquent liable to criminal prosecution. Such prosecution is not usually instituted where payment is made within the month in which liability accrues; but such leniency is at the discretion of the officers of the court.

TO CORRECT SOURNESS IN WINE. 363.

Put in a bag the root of a wild horseradish cut in bits. Let it down in the wine and leave it there two days; take it out and put in a fresh root, repeating the same until the desideratum is acquired. A bag of wheat will have the same effect where the wine is but slightly affected.

TO CURE ROPY BEER. 364.

Put a handful of flour, and the same quantity of hops, with a little powdered alum, into the beer and rummage it well

TO GIVE BEER THE APPEARANCE OF AGE. 365.

Add a few handsful of pickled cucumbers and Seville oranges, both chopped up. This will make malt liquor appear six months older than it really is.

TO NEUTRALIZE WHISKEY. 366.

To forty gallons of whiskey add one and a half pounds of unslacked lime, three-quarters of a pound of alum and half a pint of spirits of niter. Let it stand for a day or two and draw it off.

TO REDUCE HOLLAND GIN. 367.

To twenty-five gallons of pure Holland gin add twenty-five gallons or pure French spirit and half a gallon of pure sugar syrup. Mix thoroughly.

TO REMOVE ROPINESS FROM WINE. 368.

Add a little catechu or a few bruised mountain ash berries.

TO RESTORE FLAT WINE. 369.

To every hundred gallons add four or five pounds of white sugar, honey or raisins, and bung close. A little spirits may also be added.

WAX PUTTY FOR LEAKY BUNGS. 370.

Spirits of turpentine, two pounds; tallow, four pounds; solid turpentine, twelve pounds. Melt the wax and solid turpentine together over a slow fire, and then add the tallow. When melted, remove to a cool place and stir in the spirits of turpentine and allow it to cool.

VALUABLE SUGGESTIONS

Many absinthe drinkers of late have become possessed of a novel and scientific notion through the publication of a series of articles, which have appeared in a certain medical journal, claiming that, before drinking absinthe in any form, great pains should be taken to carefully pour off the top of the liquid or allow it to flow off while dripping, so that the thin scum which always floats to the top of absinthe will not be partaken of. This is said to be the only deleterious property of absinthe; and should a small quantity of this floating substance be placed in contact with any abrasion of the cuticle, serious inflammation would be the consequence, proving beyond a doubt its poisonous nature.

Another new wrinkle with absinthe drinkers is termed an Egg Suicesse. It is highly spoken of as a morning eye-opener, and is made the same as an ordinary Suicesse, with the white of an egg well shaken with the absinthe, orgeat and ice. When the syphon is turned onto this drink, a thick foam immediately collects on top of the beverage. The mouth of the syphon should then be placed below the rim of the glass and turned on again, which will cause this head to raise high above the liquid (à la Mountaineer) if the mixture is well frozen and the syphon cold. The poison spoken of in the preceding suggestion is said to adhere to the frozen egg, thereby obviating the necessity of pouring off the surface of the drink, as the beverage itself can be partaken of without quaffing the unhealthy foam.

In making a cocktail of any liquor, always strive to serve the beverage as cold as possible. Some bartenders freeze the glass in which the drink is to be served by filling it with fine ice before commencing to mix the drink. As soon as the cocktail is prepared, they throw the fine ice out of the serving glass and immediately strain the beverage from the mixer into the now frozen glass. This is a very nice and tasty way to do, but of course all this extra labor requires time, and is therefore impracticable during a rush of business.

Never try to make fancy cocktails without a special order, as they should be as plain as possible for the average lover of this popular beverage.

Do not serve a frosted glass to a gentleman who wears a mustache, as the sugar adheres to that appendage and causes great inconvenience.

The idea of making any liquor into a cocktail was conceived only for the purpose of removing the sharp, raw taste peculiar to all plain liquors; therefore it is not necessary to use a combination of cordials, essences, absinthe or lime juice as some "bar-creatures" do; but by adhering strictly to the herein contained directions you will be enabled to serve these famous American decoctions in as fine style as the highest salaried mixologist in the land.

Some of my recipes for the manufacture of cocktails order the dispenser to twist a piece of lemon peel into the glass in which the drink is to be served ; but in some establishments this is forbidden, the bartenders being ordered to twist and drop the lemon peel into the mixing glass and strain the peel with the ice when putting the drink into the serving glass. This is merely a matter of form, however, as the flavor is the same in both cases.

In place of mixing sugar and water every time a cocktail is ordered, a nice way to do is to dissolve a quantity of loaf sugar in a large vessel of hot water; strain, bottle and use, when needed for cocktails or toddies, from a bitter bottle. A few dashes of this toddy water, or whiskey gum, as it is called, is sufficient for a cocktail, and the beverage is clearer and better flavored thereby.

In making lemonades, whiskey, brandy, gin or any kind of cocktails, whiskey, brandy, white wine or imperial punches, juleps or any beverage containing any effervescent liquid, always *mix with a spoon*. *A shaker should be used only in the mixing of* frozen absinthes, milk punches, egg noggs, claret punches, fizzes, cobblers or drinks that cannot be dissolved with a spoon, or beverages that must be frozen.

In mixing hot drinks always use the thinnest of glassware of uniform thickness, and place a spoon in the glass before pouring in the hot water; then you will never be troubled with breakage.

Rinse out your glass with boiling water before commencing to make a hot drink. This enables one to serve the beverage much hotter.

Should you ever have occasion to *cool a hot drink*, never put a piece of ice in it, as this impairs the flavor. By pouring the beverage into a clean, cool glass the desired temperature will be attained in a few moments.

Before pouring liquor into a hot drink, always see that the sugar is thoroughly dissolved, because it is a difficult matter to dissolve it afterwards.

Never set a *hot drink on a polished bar top* without a saucer or a clean napkin under it, as it will surely leave a bad mark.

In making *drinks requiring a combination of sugar and lime or lemon juice*, no strict rule regarding the quantity of either sour or sweet can be adhered to, as no two tastes are exactly alike, and the quantity of juice in different lemons and limes varies. Therefore, a bartender must necessarily use his own judgment regarding the blending of these indispensible ingredients. The great trick in making punches, sours, lemonades, and all drinks necessitating the use of a mixture of sour and sweet, is to blend them so that the taste of one will be no more perceptible than the flavor of the other. This can only be acquired by practice, and is one of the most important secrets in barkeeping.

Some recipes in this book order the use of *lime juice*, and some call for *lemon juice*. Long experience has taught me that the juice of one is as good as the juice of the other; but in using *rind or peel* for a flavor, lemon peel is the proper thing, as lime-skin has a rank, bitter taste, and is therefore worthless.

When helping a customer to a still wine of any description, vermouth, a liqueur or any plain drink with which you do not wish to serve ice, a very nice and tasty way to cool the beverage is to hold a piece of ice over the serving glass with a pair of ice tongs, and pour the drink over it.

For the benefit of the novice, I will state that a *jigger* (which is ordered used in many of my recipes) is a little silver measure shaped like and having the same capacity as a sherry glass. It is supposed to hold an average drink of any liquor, and I would advise any inexperienced person to use either a jigger or a sherry glass until they accustom themselves to measuring correctly by practice with the eye.

Always use thin glassware if you wish to have your drinks appreciated; for there is an old adage known to all club-men and lovers of good things that "A drink of beer tastes as good out of a thin glass as champagne does out of a cup."

In drawing a cork from a bottle of any effervescent liquid, always hold the bottle in an oblique position, as near horizontal as possible, without getting the mouth of the bottle below the surface line of the contents. Hold the bottle in this position for a few moments before standing it up, and no waste can possibly occur. The principle of this little trick is that the bubbles formed by the sudden contact of the heavy oxygen with the lighter gas contained in the bottle rise perpendicularly; therefore, when the bottle is held in a vertical position, the first-formed globules of air containing quantities of the valuable liquid are forced through the neck of the bottle by the successive formation of others, causing loss, damage and inconvenience; but, when the bottle is held obliquely, the bubbles, still true to the same law of nature, continue the same upward course; but, instead of escaping through the opening, they are arrested by the slope of the bottle, and the gas which must necessarily escape through the only vent to relieve this pressure is not in the form of bubbles; therefore the desideratum is acquired.

In opening champagne the preceding hint is invaluable, although a corkscrew is never used for this purpose.

The proper way of opening a bottle of effervescent wine is to carefully remove the capsule covering the cork, break with a twist of a wine opener, or cut with a pair of wire nippers, the wire which holds the cork, wipe the neck of the bottle and the cork with a napkin so that no dirt can drop into the glass which you are about to serve the wine in, and keep the thumb of the left hand firmly over the cork during these preparations so that no accident can possibly happen; then firmly grasp the bottom of the bottle with the right hand, and hold the cork fast between the thumb and forefinger of the left hand, twist the bottle a few times backward and forward so as to loosen the cork, and then allow the pressure of the gas within to do the rest, taking pains to not let it do too much, and never allow any noise to be heard as the cork leaves the bottle. By holding the bottle in the position spoken of in the preceding suggestion, no danger of an overflow need be feared.

In opening a bottle of any wine or liquor of any description, always strive to *jar the contents as little as possible* so that, should there be any sediment in the bottle, it will not be served with the drink, but will remain at the bottom. A bottle of old Burgundy or fine claret is unfit for use after having been shaken just before serving; and any connoisseur's appetite for a good drink of wine or liquor is always more or less impaired by being compelled to drink any beverage which has been poured from an almost empty bottle of any wine or liquor.

The iceing of wines is of great importance; but how few bartenders pay attention to this subject? Clarets and Burgundies should never be cooled in any manner, but should be kept and drank at a temperature of about sixty degrees Fahrenheit. Hocks, Reislings and Sauternes can be kept at any temperature without injury, but it is advisable to keep them cool. Ice may be served in the glass with these wines, and the flavor will not be impaired thereby; but the flavor of champagne is always injured by serving in this manner. The proper way to treat effervescent wines is to ice the bottle well before uncorking. Cognacs should always be kept at an even temperature, as extreme heat or cold is very injurious to them; but whiskies of all kinds are much more palatable when iced, and the liquor is not impaired thereby. Malt liquors of all kinds should be served at a temperature as near fifty degrees Fahrenheit as possible.

372.

WM. T. (COCKTAIL) BOOTHBY'S
TEN COMMANDMENTS.

I.

Always be on time to relieve the other watch. It is a good plan to make a practice of arriving a few minutes early so as to arrange your toilet and step to your station on time.

II.

See that your finger nails are always clean and your person presents a tidy appearance.

III.

Always appear pleasant and obliging under all circumstances.

IV.

Avoid conversations of a religious or political nature.

V.

When going off watch always dry and polish all the glassware and tools which you have used on your watch, and see that everything is in its proper place, so that your relief can work to advantage as soon as he arrives at his post.

VI.

Sell all the liquor you can, but use as little as possible yourself.

VII.

If you are troubled with sore feet, bathe them regularly. Avoid patched or ragged hosiery, and wear a comfortable shoe with a heavy sole. Light soles, low-cut shoes or slippers should never be worn behind a bar.

VIII.

Keep the floor behind the bar as dry as possible. It not only looks better, but you will find your health greatly improved by following this rule. Many bartenders contract rheumatism, neuralgia and many other serious complaints through carelessness in this respect.

IX.

After using a bottle or tool always replace it before doing anything else. Make this a rule that should never be broken ; and, when you are rushed with business, you will never be compelled to hunt for this or that, but you will always know just where it is.

X.

After a party has finished drinking, remove the glassware from the bar as soon as possible, and dry and polish the bar top immediately, never allowing a particle of moisture to remain. This is a very important rule.

CHAMPAGNE.

The importations into this country during 1890 show **90,130** cases of G. H. MUMM & CO'S Extra Dry, being an increase of **27,000** cases over the previous year, evidencing the high appreciation in which this wine is held for its excellent quality. It is recommended by the most eminent physicians in this country for its purity, small amount of *alcohol* and wholesomeness, while for a fine dry champagne, "G. H. MUMM & CO'S EXTRA DRY" is considered by connoisseurs as unsurpassed.

Val Blatz celebrated "WIENER" Beer, Milwaukee.
"ANHEUSER" and "BUDWEISER" Lager Beer. St. Louis.
APOLLINARIS Natural Mineral Water.
HUNYADI JANOS Natural Aperient Water.

TRADE SUPPLIED BY

JONES, MUNDY & CO.,

16 Front Street, San Francisco.

HEADQUARTERS IN CALIFORNIA.

*Restaurant
a la Carte.*

THE LOUVRE

Cor. Eddy and Powell,

San Francisco, Cal.

*Separate
Dining Rooms
for Ladies.*

IMPORTED WINES AND CHAMPAGNES.

Imported Pilsen, Culmbach, Erlanger, Augustiner, Pchorr, etc., Beers.

Anheuser-Busch Brewing Association St. Louis Beer in Bulk and Bottles.

The Largest Establishment of this Kind in America.

VEUVE CLICQUOT PONSARDIN

YELLOW LABEL
DRY.

WHITE LABEL
RICH.

The Most Delicious Champagne of the Age.

A. VIGNIER, Sole Agent for the Pacific Coast,

429 & 431 Battery Street, San Francisco, Cal.

JOHN WIELAND,
FREDERICKSBURG,
CHICAGO,
UNITED STATES

CELEBRATED LAGER BEERS.

TO BE HAD EVERYWHERE.

Extra Pale, Pilsener, Culmbacher, Elk and Columbia.

PORTER and ALE.

General Office, 403 Market Street, S. F.

TELEPHONE No. 1150.

SROUFE & McCRUM,

IMPORTERS OF LIQUORS,

Fine Kentucky Whiskies, etc.

Sole Agents for "PIPIFAX" BITTERS.

208 & 210 MARKET ST. and 9 & 11 PINE ST.

SAN FRANCISCO.

A Napa Soda Lemonade is a Delicious Drink.

Sold in all Saloons, Restaurants, Drug Stores, etc., on the Pacific Coast.

ADENDA.

COCKTAILS.

Vampire

Panama Cocktail, New Orleans style.
Into a mixing glass of cracked ice pour half
a jigger of Eng. gin, half a jigger if French.
Vermuth and several drops of lime juice, shake
well, strain into stem cocktail glass and serve.

Wagner Cocktail.
One third sloe gin, one third cherry ner-
mouth and a dash of orange bitters, serve very
cold.

Affinity Cocktail, a la J.M. Brownbecell, Multnomah Hotel, Portland, Oreg.
2/5 French Vermuth, 2/5 Italian Vermuth, 1/5
Creme' de Violet. Shake well with cracked ice,
strain into cocktail glass and serve.

Rosington Cocktail.
1/3 Italian Ver mouth, 2/3 dry Eng. gin,
and 3 pieces of orange peel well shaken with
cracked ice, strained into and served in stem cockta
tailm glass.

Saratoga Cooler.
Make the same as a lemonade gut use ginger ale
instead of water. In short a Saratoga Cooler is
nothing but a ginger ale lemonade.

Duchess Cocktail, a la Bob Ipswitch, Goldfield, Nev.
1/3 Italian Vermuth, 1/3 French Vermouth, 1/3
Absinthe. Shake well with cracked ice, strain
into cocktail glass and serve. This is also called
a Loftus.

Florida Cocktail, a la Eddy Baldry, Salt Lake City.
2/3 orange juice, 1/3 Italian Vermouth, shake
well with cracked ice and serve in cocktail glass.

Pendennis Club Cocktail, Louisville, Kentucky.
1/4 French Vermouth, 1/4 Apricot Brandy, 1/2
Plymouth gin, shake well and strain.

Indian Cocktail, a le Geo.Kinsey, King Edward
Hotel, Edmonton, N.W.T.
   1/2 Sloe gin, 1/4 Italian Vermouth, 1/4 French
Vermouth and a dash of Orange bitters served cold.

Jack Rose Cocktail a la R.H.Towner, Wm.St. N.Y.
   Juice of 1 lemon, 1 part grenadine syrup, 2
parts apple jack, shake well with cocktail ice and
strain into cocktail glass.

Keeney Cocktail, a la Dr.Keeney, S.F.
   4/5 Boord's Old Tom Gin, 1/5 French Vermouth
frappe shake thoroughly with lots of cracked ice
and serve immediately.

Loftus Cocktail a la Dan Williams of the famous
Fairmont Hotel Bar.
1/3 French Vermouth, 1/3 Italian Vermouth. 1/3
Absinth shake well with cracked ice strain,serve.

Lone Tree Cocktail originated at Myopia Hunt Club,
Hamilton, Mass.   2/3 Italian Vermouth and 1/3
Plymouth Gin shake well.

Merry Widow, a la Ernest Simpson.
   1/2 Byrrh wine, 1/2 Plymouth Gin, stir well
and serve cold in stem glass.

Missippi Mail, a la Sidney Melbourne Palace Hotel
Bar, S.F.
   Shake weal together a pony of creme de menthe,
a bar spoonful of sugar, and some milk. Strain into
claret glass and serve.

Marguerite Cocktail conceived by the famous Otto
   as served in Henry's Hotel 11 Rue Volney, Paris,
   France and the La Salle Hotel, Chicago.
   Juice of 1/2 lime, grenadine, Plymouth gin,
dash of absinthe, white of ell. Shake well with
cracked ice and serve in claret glass.

Orange Blossom a la Gene Lee, Palace Hotel Bar.
   To juice of 1 orange ass a jigger of Plymouth
gin and sugar to taste,shake well with cracked ice
strain in large goblet cracked ice, fill with
seltzer water, stir well, decorate and serve.

Orange Blossom Cocktail, a la Eddy Rogers,.....
  Seattle, Wash.
Half fresh orange juice and half Plymouth Gin.
Shake together with cracked ice.

Orange Glory, Same as orange Blossom with white
of egg added.

Opalescent Cocktail a la Bingham American Congress
Bar, City of Mexico.
    Juice of 1/2 lemon, grenadine to taste, 1 leaf
of mint, white of an egg, Plymouth Gin. Shake and
strain into claret glass.

Champagne Cup a la Geo.Suff,Palace Hotel, S.F.
  Cook fresh sliced pineapple in pint of white
wine about 4 hours. Peeled peaches may be used
instead, when in season. Then add a flavor of
Batavia Arrac and Champagne in proportion, sevee
ice cold

Apple Hammer, a la Eddie Hammer.
1/2 Plymouth gin, 1/2 Cinzano Italian Vermouth,
juice of 1 lime, bottle of Club Soda. Serve in
pint glasses with a bottle of Club Soda and a
lump of ice-stir well.

Stinger, a la J.C. O'Connor proprietor of the
handsomest cafe for gentlemen in the world , corner Eddy & Market Sts. S.F., Calif.
1/4 white creme de menthe and 3/4 eeng gpgnac.
Shake well and serve cold in sherry glass.

Gin Daisy, a la Mike Fitspatrick,Butler Hotel,
Vancouver, B.C.
  A pony raspberry syrup, a pony lemon juice, a
jigger of Plymouth Gin and some effervescent water
Stir thoroughly.Pour ingo a punch glass containing some cracked ice,decorate with fruits and
serve with straws. A whiskey daisy is made by
using shisky instead of gin.

Ramos Fizz New Orleans style.

In order to concoct this famous beverage a
batter must first be prepared as follows;
To the well beaten whites of any number of eggs
stir in as much bar sugar as the eggs will take up
making a thick paste. This paste is then flavored
to taste with French Orange Flower Water and
placed in some glass or porcelaine vessel and
kept cool and covered.
When desirous of brewing a Ramos Fizz place
a heaping barspoonful of the batter in a mixing
glass, add enough lemon or lime juice to overcome
the sweetness of the batter, a jigger of good
English Gin, a piece of twisted lemon peel and a
table spoonful of rich cream.
Shake thoroughly with some cracked ice,strain
into a cut goblet, fill up with cold effervescent
water and serve.

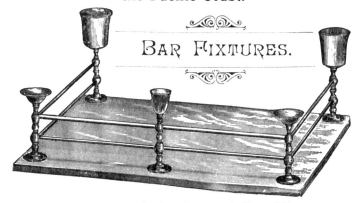

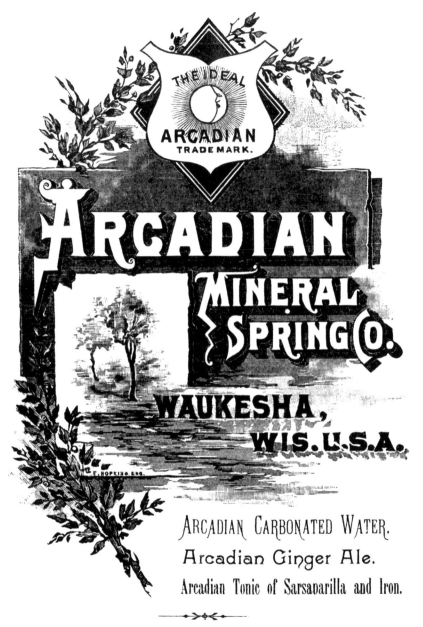

THE IDEAL
ARCADIAN
TRADE MARK.

ARCADIAN
MINERAL SPRING CO.
WAUKESHA, WIS. U.S.A.

E. HOPKINS, ENG.

ARCADIAN CARBONATED WATER.

Arcadian Ginger Ale.

Arcadian Tonic of Sarsaparilla and Iron.

JOHNSON LOCKE MERCANTILE CO., San Francisco, Sole Agents.

TUCKED INTO A RARE COPY OF THE 1900 EDITION
of Boothby's book is a handwritten sixteen-page "ADDENDA."
The recipes, written in pencil and ink by an unknown hand
or hands, are remarkably similar to the typed recipes that we
found tipped into the California Historical Society's even
rarer copy of Boothby's 1891 edition. Like cocktail papyri,
these ancient pages are as enigmatic as they are illuminating.
It is likely that they were written after 1908. They include
a page number and a recipe number from the 1908 edition,
for example, as well as references to Chicago's LaSalle Hotel,
which opened in 1909, and John Charles O'Connor's bar,
which did not appear in the San Francisco city directory
until 1909. We offer them here—courtesy of mixologist
John C. Burton—for comparison with the typed pages.
Beneath each handwritten page, we have included relevant
entries from the 1908 edition of Boothby's book. Those
with an asterisk are from *its* addenda, entitled "Some
New-Up-To-Now Seductive American Cocktails."

ADDENDA —

VAMPIRE COCKTAIL

Into a mixing Glass of cracked ice pour half a jigger of English gin, half a jigger of French Vermouth and several drops of lime juice, shake well strain into a stem cocktail glass and serve

Wagner Cocktail
One third sloe gin
One third Cherry brandy
One third Italian Vermouth
and a dash of Orange bitters
serve very cold

*VAMPIRE COCKTAIL.
Half Coates Plymouth gin and half French Vermouth, with several drops of lime juice added.

*WAGNER COCKTAIL.
One-third Sloe gin, one-third Cherry brandy, one-third Cinzano (Italian) Vermouth, one dash of Orange bitters. Serve very cold.

— ADDENDA —

The man who keeps his mouth shut has the rest of us guessing.

Victor Reiter.

Affinity Cocktail
a la J. M. Brownell. Multnomah Hotel
Portland, Oregon.

Two-fifths French Vermouth
Two-fifths Italian Vermouth
One fifth Crème de Violette.
Shake well with cracked ice
Strain into Cocktail Glass + serve.

*AFFINITY COCKTAIL.

Frappé two-fifths French Vermouth, two-fifths Italian (Cinzano) Vermouth and one-fifth Crème de Violette. Serve in chilled stem cocktail glasses.

[Victor M. Reiter came to San Francisco after a stint as head caterer at New York's Delmonico's. In 1912, after more than twenty years as the Palace Hotel's maître d'hôtel, he became general manager of Hotel Oakland, near Lake Merritt.—Ed.]

— ADDENDA —

Rossington Cocktail

One Third Italian Vermouth, Two Thirds dry English gin and three pieces of orange peel well shaken with cracked ice strained into and served in a stem cocktail glass

Saratoga Cooler

Make the same as a lemonade but use ginger ale instead of water. In short a Saratoga Cooler is nothing more than a ginger ale lemonade

---

*ROSSINGTON COCKTAIL.
One-third Cinzano Italian Vermouth, two-thirds Coates Plymouth gin,
and three pieces of orange peel; frappé, strain; serve in stem Cocktail glass.

PLAIN LEMONADE.
Into a large mixing-glass place a tablespoonful of bar sugar, the juice of
two lemons and just enough water to dissolve the sugar, stir thoroughly and pour into a large goblet
containing a piece of ice, fill the goblet with water, stir, decorate, and serve with straws.

- ADDENDA -

Duchess Cocktail
a la Bob IPSWITCH   GOLDFIELD, NEV.
One-Third Italian Vermouth
One-Third French Vermouth
One-Third Absinthe
Shake well with cracked ice
strain into cocktail glass
and - serve.
This well known appetizer
is also called a Loftus.

Florida Cocktail
a la Eddy Baldry - Salt Lake City.
Two-thirds orange juice
One-third Italian Vermouth
Shake well with cracked
ice and serve in cocktail
glass

*DUCHESS COCKTAIL.
Frappé equal parts of (Cinzano) Italian Vermouth, Absinthe and French Vermouth.
Serve in stem glasses.

*FLORIDA COCKTAIL.
Two-thirds orange juice and one-third Coates Plymouth gin; frappé,
and serve in stem Cocktail glass.

In dennis Club cocktail
Louisville, Kentucky.
One quarter French Vermouth
One Quarter Apricot Brandy
One Half Plymouth gin
shake well and strain

Pineapple Bronx
a la Frank H. DORAN   SAN FRANCISCO
Known also as a Carley
cocktail. In some sections
it is called a Queen Cocktail
Proceed exactly as in the
mixing of a Bronx cocktail
but substitute some sliced
pineapple instead of pieces
of orange.

---

*PENDENNIS CLUB COCKTAIL.

(Louisville, KY.) One-quarter Apricot brandy,
one-quarter French Vermouth, one-half Coates
Plymouth gin; shake well, and serve very cold.

*PINEAPPLE BRONX.

(Called sometimes Queen Cocktail.) Proceed exactly
as in the mixing of a Bronx Cocktail, but substitute
some sliced pineapple instead of pieces of orange.

*BRONX COCKTAIL.

Cut up one-sixth of a nice ripe orange into small
cubes, skin and all; place in a large mixing glass;
add one-third jigger of Coates Plymouth gin,
one-third jigger of Italian (Cinzano) Vermouth,
and one-third jigger of French Vermouth.
Shake well with cracked ice, strain through a fine
strainer into a chilled Cocktail glass, and serve.

a Indian Cocktail
a la Geo. Kinsey, King Edward Hotel
Edmonton
N.W.T.
One-half Sloe Gin
One-quarter Italian Vermouth
One-quarter French Vermouth
and a dash of orange bitters
served very cold.

Inter State
A pousse café glass of brown
curacao with cream on top.

Jack Rose Cocktail
a la R. H. Towner
62 William St. N.Y.
Juice of one lemon
1 part grenadine syrup
2 parts apple jack
shake well with cracked ice
and strain into cocktail glass

---

*INDIAN COCKTAIL. One-half Sloe gin, one-quarter Cinzano Italian Vermouth, one-quarter French Vermouth, and a dash of Orange bitters; serve very cold.

*JACK ROSE COCKTAIL.
(a la R. H. Townes, 62 William St., New York.) The juice of one lemon, one part Grenadine syrup, and two parts Apple Jack. Shake well with cracked ice, and strain into Cocktail glass.

BROWN SHAKE
Into a small mixing-glass place three-quarters of a sherry glassful of brown Curaçao, a barspoonful of sour and two drops of Angostura bitters.
Into a shaker place two or three lumps of ice and shake thoroughly. Strain into a sherry glass and serve.

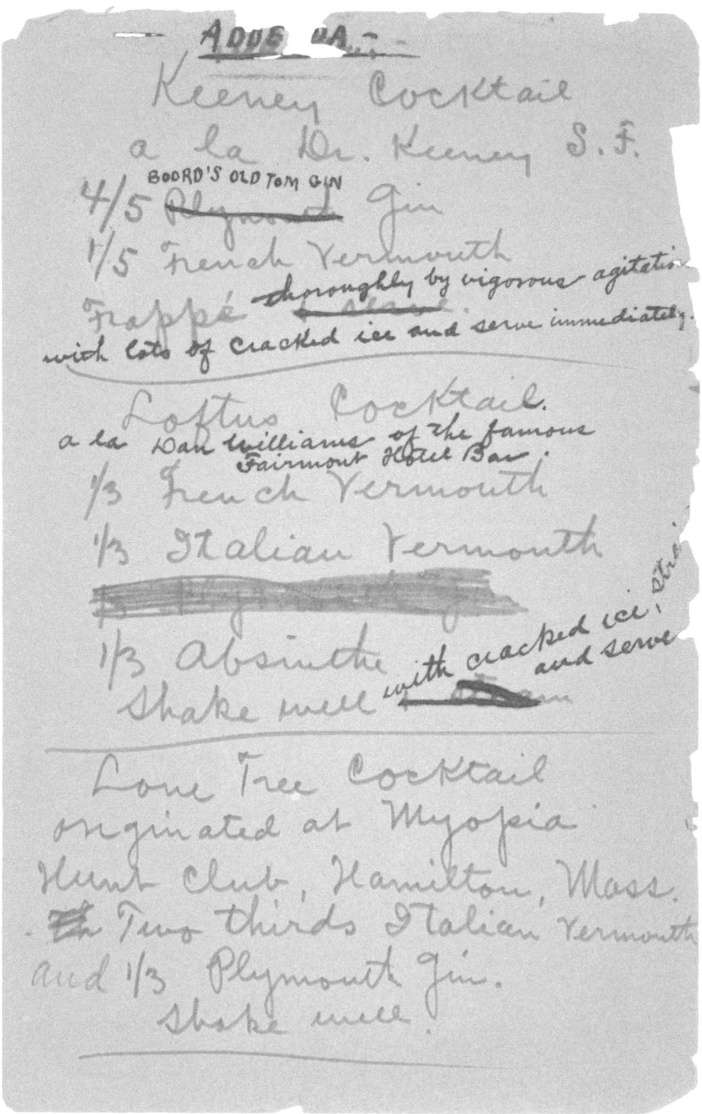

Handwritten note (facsimile):

ADDENDA.

Keeney Cocktail
a la Dr. Keeney S.F.
4/5 BOORD'S OLD TOM GIN ~~Plymouth~~ Gin
1/5 French Vermouth
Frappé thoroughly by vigorous agitation
with lots of cracked ice and serve immediately.

Loftus Cocktail.
a la Dan Williams of the famous
Fairmount Hotel Bar.
1/3 French Vermouth
1/3 Italian Vermouth
1/3 Absinthe with cracked ice, strain
Shake well and serve

Lone Tree Cocktail
originated at Myopia
Hunt Club, Hamilton, Mass.
Two thirds Italian Vermouth
and 1/3 Plymouth gin.
Shake well.

---

*KEENEY COCKTAIL.
Four-fifths Old Tom Cordial gin,
one-fifth French Vermouth; shake
thoroughly with plenty of cracked ice
in a large mixing-glass. Serve before
the mixture becomes clear.

[In 1909, the year that the new Palace Hotel
opened, Dr. James W. Keeney was practicing
medicine nearby, at 240 Stockton.—Ed.]

*LOFTUS COCKTAIL. One-third French Vermouth,
one-third Cinzano Italian Vermouth, and one-third Absinthe.
Shake well with cracked ice, and serve in stem glass.

*LONE TREE COCKTAIL.
(Originated at Myopia Hunt Club, Hamilton, Mass.)
One-third Coates Plymouth gin and two-thirds Cinzano
Italian Vermouth; chill thoroughly, and serve
in stem Cocktail glass.

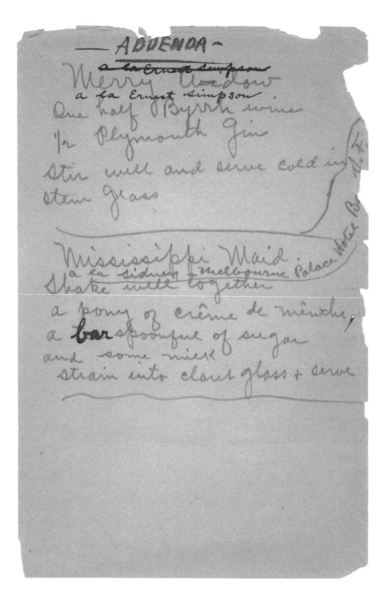

*MERRY WIDOW COCKTAIL.
Frappé thoroughly equal parts of Byrrh wine and Coates Plymouth gin,
and serve in chilled Cocktail glasses.

GRASSHOPPER.
(a la Harry O'Brien, late of the Palace Hotel, San Francisco.)
Fill a pony-glass with equal parts of Crême de Cacao and Crême de Mênthe
and see that the Crême de Cacao lies on top of the Crême de Mênthe without mixing.
[Boothby's typesettter bungled this recipe's word order. It has been corrected here.—Ed.]

— ADDENDA —

Marguerite Cocktail
Conceived by the famous Otto
as served in Henry's Hotel
#11 Rue Volney
Paris, France and the
La Salle Hotel, Chicago
Juice of half a lime
Grenadine
Plymouth gin
dash of absinthe
white of an egg
shake well with cracked ice
strain and serve in claret glass

Orange Blossom
a la Gene Lee
Palace Hotel Bar, San Francisco
To the juice of one orange, add
a jigger of Plymouth Gin
and sugar to taste; shake well
with cracked ice; strain into a
large goblet of ice, fill with seltzer,
stir well, decorate and serve with
straws.

*MARGUERITE COCKTAIL.

(Conceived by the famous "Otto" of Henry's Hotel, No. 11 Rue Volney, Paris, France, and popularized in America by the LaSalle Hotel Bar, Chicago.)
Into a large mixing-glass of cracked ice place the juice of one-half lime, just enough Grenadine to overcome the acidity of the lime juice, a jigger of Coates Plymouth gin, a dash of Absinthe, and the white of an egg; shake well, strain, and serve in claret glass.

*ORANGE BLOSSOM COCKTAIL.
Half orange juice and
half Coates Plymouth gin; frappé.

[Chicago's Hotel LaSalle, at the corner of LaSalle and Madison, opened in 1909.—Ed.]

Orange Blossom Cocktail
a la Eddy Rogers Seattle, W
Half fresh orange juice
and half Plymouth gin
shaken together with cracked
ice

Orange Glory

Same as Orange Blossom
with the white of an egg
added

Opalescent Cocktail
a la Artic Bingham   American congress bar
— City of Mexico —
Juice of 1/2 lemon
Grenadine to Taste
1 leaf of mint
white of an egg
Plymouth gin — shake well and strain into claret glass

*ORANGE GLORY COCKTAIL.
Make the same as Orange Blossom with half of the white of an egg added.

*OPALESCENT COCKTAIL.
(a la Joe Terry.)
Juice of half a lemon, Grenadine to taste, one leaf of mint,
white of half an egg, one jigger of Coates Plymouth gin;
shake well with cracked ice, strain into a small claret glass, and serve.

Champagne cup
a la Geo Supt
Palace Hotel Bar, San Francisco

Soak fresh sliced pineapple
in pint of white wine
about four hours;
peeled peaches may be used
instead, when in season.
Then add a flavor of
Batavia Arrac and Champagne
in proportion — Serve very
cold.

CHAMPAGNE CUP.
(a la Ariadne.)
Bottle of iced champagne, gill of Amontillado, liqueur glass of citronelle or maraschino,
juice and paring of an orange or lemon rubbed on sugar, verbena and cucumber;
sugar to taste and a siphon of seltzer cold.

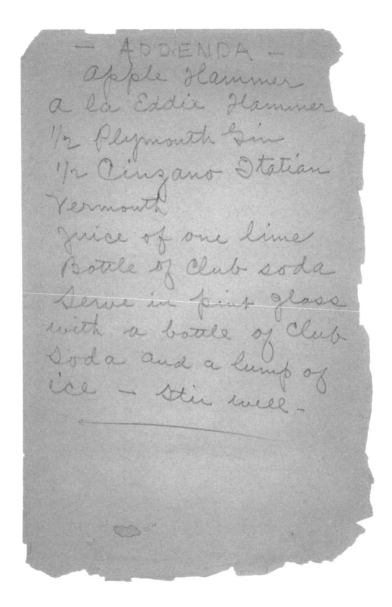

— ADDENDA —

apple Hammer
a la Eddie Hammer
1/2 Plymouth Gin
1/2 Cinzano Italian
Vermouth
Juice of one lime
Bottle of club soda
Serve in pint glass
with a bottle of club
soda and a lump of
ice — Stir well —

GIN AND SODA.

Place a long, thin glass in front of the patron into which you have placed a piece of ice;
hand out the desired brand of gin and after the guest has helped himself,
fill the glass with seltzer, and serve.

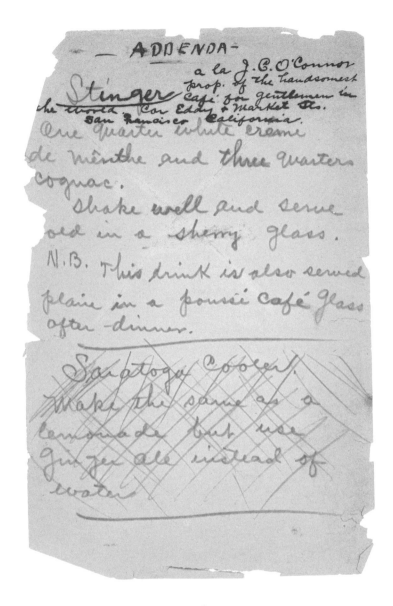

— — ADDENDA —

Stinger a la J.C. O'Connor prop. of the handsomest café for gentlemen in the world. Cor Eddy + Market Sts. San Francisco California.

One quarter white creme de mênthe and three quarters cognac.

Shake well and serve out in a sherry glass.

N.B. This drink is also served plain in a poussé café glass after-dinner.

Saratoga Cooler. Make the same as a lemonade but use ginger ale instead of water.

POUSSE CAFÉ. *(Five colors.)*

Pour the following liqueurs down the side of a small pony or pousse café glass slowly and carefully, so the ingredients will not run together but lie on top of one another without mixing.

One-fifth glassful of raspberry syrup, Crême de Vanilla or Crême de Cassis, one-fifth glassful of maraschino, one-fifth glassful of Crême de Mênthe, one-fifth glassful of yellow Chartreuse and one-fifth glassful of cognac. Serve ice water on the side.

[The Pousse Café is also known as the Stars and Stripes. Before partaking of it, one observes the beautiful stripes. After a couple of glasses, all one sees are stars. See recipe #203.—Ed.]

Gin Daisy

a la mike Fitzpatrick - Boxter Hotel -
Vancouver B.C.
a pony of raspberry syrup,
a pony of lemon juice,
a jigger of Plymouth gin
and some effervescent water
stir thoroughly. Pour into
a punch glass containing som
cracked ice, decorate with
fruits and serve with straws

P.S. A Whiskey Daisy is
made by substituting whisk
for gin. Brandy or Rum is
sometimes Also called for occa
sionally

BRANDY DAISY.
Half fill a medium-sized mixing-glass with cracked ice,
add the juice of one lemon, three dashes of orange cordial and a jigger of brandy.
Shake, strain into a punch-glass, fill up with siphon seltzer and serve.

RAMOS FIZZ
NEW ORLEANS STYLE.

In order to concoct this famous beverage a batter must first be prepared as follows. To the well beaten whites of any number of eggs stir in as much bar sugar as the eggs will take up, making a thick paste. This paste is then flavored to taste with imported French Orange Flower Water, and placed in some glass or porcelain vessel and kept cool and covered. When desirous of brewing a Ramos fizz, place a heaping barspoonful of batter in a mixing glass, add enough lemon or lime juice to overcome the sweetness of the batter, a jigger of good English Gin, a piece of twisted lemon peel and a table spoonful of rich cream. Shake thoroughly with some cracked ice, strain into a cut goblet, fill up with cold effervescent water — and serve.

NEW ORLEANS FIZZ.

Place two barspoonfuls of sour into a highball glass with a piece of ice and a jigger of gin; fill or nearly fill the glass with siphon seltzer; then add a heaping barspoonful of sugar and stir briskly. This beverage should be partaken of while effervescing.

SAZERAC COCKTAIL 63

New Orleans style
a la Armand Regnier

'nappé an old fashioned cocktail glass with shaved ice and
set it on the bar.

Then place some cracked ice
in a large mixing glass and
add a dash of gum syrup,
a jigger of good cognac
and two dashes of PEYCHAUD'S
aromatic Bitter Cordial
(a New Orleans product)
Stir thoroughly, throw the
fine ice out of the serving
glass, and rinse the same
with a few dashes of absinthe
throw out the absinthe and
then strain the cocktail into
the serving glass, add a piece
of twisted lemon peel and
serve with ice water
on the side.

SAZERAC COCKTAIL.
(a la Armand Regnier, New Orleans, LA.)
Into a mixing-glass full of cracked ice place about a small barspoonful of gum syrup,
three drops of Selner bitters and a jigger of Sazerac brandy; stir well, strain into a stem cocktail-glass
which has been rinsed out with a dash of absinthe, squeeze a piece of lemon peel
over the top and serve with ice water on the side.

[The numbers 29 and 63 (handwritten, top right) are the page and recipe numbers,
respectively, of the Regnier Sazerac Cocktail as it appears in Boothby's 1908 book.
On the same page, Boothby also shares the recipe for a Tin Roof Cocktail:
"A Tin Roof Cocktail is one that's 'on the house.'"—Ed.]

*SAZERAC COCKTAIL.
(The drink that made New Orleans famous.)
(From the recipe of the late Tom Handy, ex-manager of the world-renowned Sazerac Bar.)
Frappé an old-fashioned flat bar glass; then take a mixing glass and muddle half a cube of sugar
with a little water; add some ice, a jigger of good whiskey, two dashes of Peychaud bitters,
and a piece of twisted lemon peel; stir well until cold, then throw the ice out of the bar glass,
dash several drops of Absinthe into the same, and rinse well with the Absinthe.
Now strain the Cocktail into the frozen glass, and serve with ice water on the side.

[A careful review of the typed addenda pasted into the 1891 edition,
the handwritten addenda tucked into the 1900 edition, and the printed but
un-page-numbered addenda ("Some New-Up-To-Now Seductive American Cocktails")
in the 1908 edition suggests that Boothby reprinted his 1908 edition, using
the original printing plates and simply adding a new cover and
"new-up-to-now" recipes. One of these new recipes is for
Frank G. Doran's Exposition Cocktail: "One-third Cherry brandy, one-third
French Vermouth, and one-third Sloe gin; frappé, and serve in stem Cocktail glass."
By 1914, after several years as bartender and clerk, Doran was managing
John C. O'Connor's "café for gentlemen" at Eddy and Market.
Perhaps Doran created his Exposition Cocktail—and Boothby his new edition—
for the 1915 Panama-Pacific International Exposition. Cheers!—Ed.]

TRADITIONAL — POT DISTILLED

THE ANCHOR DISTILLING COMPANY,
established in 1993, is dedicated to creating very small batches
of traditionally distilled spirits of many types and styles.
We also experiment with completely new products from time to time.

Junípero Gin is made by hand in the classic "distilled dry gin" tradition, utilizing more than a dozen botanicals in their natural state, in a small copper pot still at our little distillery on Potrero Hill in San Francisco. The history of gin goes back at least to the mid-1600s in Holland, but its true antecedents are much earlier, those first experiments in the ancient and mysterious art of distilling in the presence of herbs and spices. The predominant flavor and aroma of a modern gin will always come from juniper (dried berries of the "common juniper," *Juniperus communis*). But the wonderful challenge for the distiller is in selecting and blending from a wide variety of additional, exotic botanicals in order to impart a uniquely satisfying, balanced character to his gin. At Anchor Distilling, we have taken delight in the adventure of researching and experimenting with many such botanicals. Our final formula must remain a secret, but we hope you will agree that we have achieved a distinctive, intriguing complexity in our Junípero Gin: light and crisp and clean, combining a deep and mysterious spiciness with subtle delicacy.

GENEVIEVE
GENEVER-*Style* GIN

G ENEVIEVE® GENEVER-STYLE GIN is an offshoot of our research into the history and evolving production methods that led to modern gin. In the late 19th century, technological advances enabled distillers to produce neutral spirits at very high proofs. When re-distilled with complex blends of juniper berries and other natural botanicals, these neutral spirits were transformed into what we know today as modern

"distilled dry gin." The earliest gins, however—which came to be known as "genever" (or "Geneva gin," or "Hollands gin," or "Schiedam-style gin")—were a very different product. To be sure, juniper berries and other botanicals are used in both styles, but 17th-century "genever" gin was distilled in primitive pot stills from a grain mash. Genevieve is our attempt to re-create this ancient and mysterious gin style. We use a grain mash of wheat, barley, and rye malts, which is distilled in a traditional copper pot still with the same botanicals we use in our modern "distilled dry gin," Junípero Gin. We hope you will enjoy comparing these two unique products, the alpha and omega of the gin story.

Many early cocktail recipes that call for "gin" actually mean "genever gin," which has a strong flavor profile because it is pot distilled from a grain mash. We encourage you to experiment and let us know about any recipes you think are a success. Of course, the most common way to consume genever has always been straight: either chilled, over ice, or—best of all— shaken with ice. A slight haze may form, which is normal for this all-natural product.

GENEVIEVE (GENEVER-STYLE GIN, 47.3% ALC/VOL (94.6 PROOF), IS DISTILLED AND BOTTLED BY ANCHOR DISTILLING COMPANY, SAN FRANCISCO, CA

OLD POTRERO®
SINGLE MALT
WHISKEY
18TH CENTURY STYLE

O LD POTRERO® 18TH-CENTURY-STYLE WHISKEY is our attempt to re-create the original whiskey of America. It is distilled in a small copper pot still at our distillery on San Francisco's Potrero Hill, from a mash of 100% rye malt. Rye was the grain of choice for America's first distillers, and using a mash of 100% rye malt produces a uniquely American whiskey.

We have found that handmade oak barrels—lightly toasted in the traditional manner—impart a wonderfully subtle flavor to our 18th-century-style American whiskey. In the 18th century, barrels were made by heating the staves over a fire of oak chips, allowing them to be bent and formed into a barrel shape. During this process, the inside of the barrel would become toasted—but not charred. For aging, we use uncharred oak barrels—both new and used. For bottling, we choose from several barrels in order to achieve a blend of balanced complexity that expresses Old Potrero Single Malt Whiskey's traditional heritage.

OLD POTRERO®

SINGLE MALT
STRAIGHT RYE
WHISKEY

19TH CENTURY STYLE

OLD POTRERO® SINGLE MALT STRAIGHT RYE WHISKEY is a part of our endeavor to re-create the original whiskey of America. It is distilled in a small copper pot still at our distillery on San Francisco's Potrero Hill, from a mash of 100% rye malt. Rye was the grain of choice for America's first distillers, and using a mash of 100% rye malt produces a uniquely

American whiskey.

Our straight rye whiskey is aged in new handmade charred oak barrels. In traditional barrel making, the cooper heats the staves over a fire of oak chips, allowing them to be bent and formed into a barrel. During this process, the inside of the barrel becomes lightly toasted. By the early 19th century, coopers had learned that if they allowed the heat to continue, the inside of the barrel would burst into flames and become charred. At Anchor, we have found that handmade oak barrels—charred in this traditional manner— impart a rich color and unique character to our rye whiskey. We hope you will enjoy comparing it with our other products. 🏴⚓

OLD POTRERO
SINGLE MALT
HOTALING'S
WHISKEY

OLD POTRERO® SINGLE MALT HOTALING'S® WHISKEY, 50% ALC/VOL. (100 PROOF). IS DISTILLED, AGED, AND BOTTLED BY ANCHOR DISTILLING COMPANY, SAN FRANCISCO, CA. BOTTLED IN BOND

THE DISTILLERS AT ANCHOR present this whiskey in commemoration of the 1906 San Francisco Earthquake and Fire, and in celebration of our indomitable city's rebirth. Our Hotaling's® Whiskey is aged in once-used, charred oak whiskey barrels.

In 1906, earthquake, fire, and dynamite ravaged nearly 4.7 square miles of San Francisco, a swath of destruction that claimed 28,188 buildings and an incalculable number of lives. After the disaster, several clergymen asserted that the catastrophe had been divine retribution, visited upon the city by the bay for its wicked ways.

Thanks in no small part to the pluck, resolve, and ingenuity of its staff, however, A. P. Hotaling & Co.'s Jackson Street whiskey warehouse survived. And so, "while millions of dollars worth of normally non-inflammable material was reduced to ashes," as the *Argonaut* would later report, thousands of "barrels of highly inflammable whisky were preserved intact in the heart of the tremendous holocaust."

After the fire, UC Berkeley professor Jerome Barker Landfield bumped into poet and wit Charles Kellogg Field. "He accompanied me to Berkeley," Landfield recalled, "and I put him up at the Faculty Club for the night. As we walked down to the station on our way back to San Francisco, Field asked me for a blank piece of paper on which to write. I handed him a used envelope. On the back he penned these lines:

'If, as they say, God spanked the town
For being over frisky,
Why did He burn the churches down
And save Hotaling's whiskey?'"